MW01029372

QUOTES
FOR THE JOURNEY

WISDOM
FOR THE WAY

COMPILED BY

GORDON S. JACKSON

NAVPRESS
BRINGING TRUTH TO LIFE
P.O. Box 35001, Colorado Springs, Colorado 80935

OUR GUARANTEE TO YOU

We believe so strongly in the message of our books that we are making this quality guarantee to you. If for any reason you are disappointed with the content of this book, return the title page to us with your name and address and we will refund to you the list price of the book. To help us serve you better, please briefly describe why you were disappointed. Mail your refund request to: NavPress, P.O. Box 35002, Colorado Springs, CO 80935.

The Navigators is an international Christian organization. Our mission is to reach, disciple, and equip people to know Christ and to make Him known through successive generations. We envision multitudes of diverse people in the United States and every other nation who have a passionate love for Christ, live a lifestyle of sharing Christ's love, and multiply spiritual laborers among those without Christ.

NavPress is the publishing ministry of The Navigators. NavPress publications help believers learn biblical truth and apply what they learn to their lives and ministries. Our mission is to stimulate spiritual formation among our readers.

Library of Congress Catalog Card Number: 99-049533
ISBN 1-57683-152-3

Cover design by Dan Jamison
Photo by Dan Wilby/Dan Wilby Photography, Inc.
Creative Team: Jacqueline Blakely, Lori Mitchell, Tim Howard, David Utley Designs

The Scripture quotation in the introduction is taken from the New American Standard Bible (NASB), © The Lockman Foundation 1960, 1962, 1963, 1968, 1971, 1972, 1973, 1975, 1977. The other version used is the HOLY BIBLE: NEW INTERNATIONAL VERSION ® (NIV®). Copyright © 1973, 1978, 1984 by International Bible Society. Used by permission of Zondervan Publishing House. All rights reserved.

Jackson, Gordon, 1949–
     Quotes for the journey, wisdom for the way / Gordon S. Jackson.
          p.   cm.
     ISBN 1-57683-152-3 (hardcover)
          1. Christian life—Quotations, maxims, etc.   I. Title.
     BV4513.J33 1999
     242—dc21
                                                                        99-049533

Printed in the United States of America

1 2 3 4 5 6 7 8 9 10 11 12 13 14 15 / 03 02 01 00

INTRODUCTION

Nothing can replace the Bible's importance as the touch-stone and roadmap for committed Christian living. But Christians who take their faith seriously draw on additional sources to shape their faith journeys: the local church, good pastoring, caring friends and family, personal devotions, and good books, among others. All can point us to Christ and, like Scripture itself, are "profitable for teaching, for reproof, for correction, for training in righteousness" (2 Timothy 3:16). All these sources can serve as markers along the road.

This anthology of quotations offers one such set of markers. Each quotation contained here is designed to help direct us on our Christian journey—encouraging us when we're heading in the right direction, warning us when we're about to make a wrong turn or stray off track, or pointing out important information along the way.

These quotations were selected to meet four standards. The first is that they flow from and are faithful to a Christian worldview. The overwhelming majority are from Christians. Many are from contemporary sources, but they are drawn from Christians throughout history. These sources represent a wide range of theological traditions. Some quotations draw upon the Jewish roots of our faith. Others are from sources that are not explicitly Christian, or are even hostile to Christianity or the church. These are included because each has something particularly provocative, challenging, or ironic to offer. But whatever the source, each quote was selected because I believe it offers some kind of lesson to Christians who take their faith seriously.

Second, I wanted the quotations to be highly applicable to day-to-day discipleship and to practical Christian living. This collection was intentionally limited to topics or concepts that are likely to characterize the walk and talk of ordinary Christians.

Third, each quotation was selected because of its uniqueness: in its message, its creativity, its capacity to stretch our thinking. I can readily imagine each entry being used by a Christian friend, teacher, pastor, parent, speaker, or newsletter writer, who says something like, "You know, that reminds me of what C. S. Lewis said about our Christian giving . . ." or "what D. L. Moody said about evangelism. . . ." I wanted each quote to be meaningful enough—given the right circumstances—for you to want to quote it to someone else as an encouragement or warning, or to make a teaching point.

Finally, I wanted the quotations to be highly readable; provocative and thoughtful, without being offensive; and fresh and full of surprises.

The quotations are arranged by topic. An author index is included at the end of the book. Inevitably, some overlap exists between different topics, but I have tried to place quotations in the category that seemed their most likely primary home. Selecting the topics and quotations was, of course, a purely subjective exercise; my objective was to include a wide range of topics, rather than strive for any selection pretending to be definitive. Similarly, the quotations included here were chosen for their various voices and views.

One weakness marking this volume is that the quotations are heavily dominated by western, particularly British and U.S., sources. This is not because only British and American Christians have anything worth saying; on the contrary, members of the Christian family around the world have much to share. However, finding quotations from nonwestern sources was more difficult. Similarly, most of the quotes are from men, reflecting the reality that male voices have dominated the church since its inception. Also, many quotations contain references to "man," "men," "mankind," or similar generic references to people. As products of an earlier era, these quotations lack the inclusive language that increasingly marks contemporary English. In keeping with a concern to record all quotations accurately, these were included unchanged. When it seemed necessary, brief identifications, explanations, or dates were provided.

This compilation of quotations is indebted to scores of similar anthologies and other books and magazines, from which I have drawn in varying degrees to supplement my own collection of quotations that I have compiled over the past several decades. The most important resources included:

Christianity Today

A Dictionary of Religious and Spiritual Quotations
by Geoffrey Parrinder

Dictionary of Quotations by Bergen Evans

Great Quotes and Illustrations by George Sweeting

Holy Humor by Cal and Rose Samra

Illustrations Unlimited by James S. Hewett

The Joyful Noiseletter

Leo Rosten's Treasury of Jewish Quotations by Leo Rosten

The Macmillan Dictionary of Religious Quotations
by Margaret Pepper

The New Book of Christian Quotations by Tony Castle

The Oxford Dictionary of Quotations, third edition

Peter's Quotations: Ideas for our Time
by Laurence J. Peter

Quotable Saints by Rhonda De Sola Chervin

Simpson's Contemporary Quotations by James B.
Simpson

The Topical Encyclopedia of Living Quotations
by Sherwood Eliot Wirt and Kersten Beckstrom

A Treasury of Quotations on Christian Themes
by Carroll E. Simcox

The Treasury of Religious & Spiritual Quotations
by Rebecca Davison and Susan Mesner

The Whole World Book of Quotations
by Kathryn Petras and Ross Petras

The Wittenburg Door (subsequently *The Door*)

The World Treasury of Religious Quotations
by Ralph Woods

12,000 Religious Quotations by Frank S. Mead

I have tried to be as accurate as possible in gathering the entries included here. However, it often is difficult to track down the original authorship of a particular statement or to be certain you have the original wording. Not surprisingly, particularly memorable expressions often get attributed to more than one source—something I have noted where necessary. I apologize for whatever inaccuracies have crept into the collection, either through my own errors or those in the works of others on which I have relied.

Whether you use this anthology as a reference tool, for quotations on a particular topic, for a word to include in an encouraging note to a friend, or simply for browsing, I hope that the quotations that follow will in some modest way enrich your own faith journey or the Christian walk of those whose lives you touch.

ACKNOWLEDGMENTS

I am indebted to many individuals, in particular the friends and colleagues at Whitworth College and Whitworth Community Presbyterian Church in Spokane, Washington, who helped shaped this manuscript in various ways. They include Laura Bloxham, Al Gray, Tim Harrison, Claude Matterson, Terry McGonigal, Eric Peterson, Ron Pyle, JoAnn Verhey, and John Walker. Special thanks are due to Jim Edwards and Karen Harrison for their helpful comments on the manuscript; to Jim Singleton for his exceptional help in locating quotations; and to Gail Fielding for her inventive persistence in tracking down interlibrary loan materials.

Ruth Denny, also of Spokane, graciously gave me access to the library of her late husband Randy. I greatly regret that I never had the opportunity to meet him.

As noted in the Introduction, this anthology draws from many similar works. I am particularly indebted to the collections listed there.

Finally, a thank you to my family for their patience and encouragement as I plodded through this work and for their help with some of the humdrum tasks that this project entailed. My daughter Sarah merits particular mention for her editorial assistance.

TOPICS

TOPICS

QUOTES
FOR THE JOURNEY

———————

WISDOM
FOR THE WAY

ANXIETY, DESPAIR, & WORRY ➳

In the arid times, the best thing to do is to go on with the habits of the Christian life and of the church. If we do, we can be sure that the sun will shine again.
— WILLIAM BARCLAY

Never despair; but if you do, work on in despair.
— EDMUND BURKE

When you are in the dark, listen, and God will give you a very precious message for someone else when you get into the light.
— OSWALD CHAMBERS

The evil one is pleased with sadness and melancholy.
— ST. FRANCIS DE SALES

Don't worry about the future—worry quenches the work of grace within you. The future belongs to God. He is in charge of all things. Never second-guess him.
— FRANÇOIS FÉNELON

It is quite possible to fear, obey, trust, and rely upon the Lord and still "walk in darkness and have no light." [Isaiah 50:10] You are living in obedience but have entered a dark night of the soul.
— RICHARD FOSTER

Anxiety is the natural result when our hopes are centered in anything short of God and his will for us.
— BILLY GRAHAM

The sovereign cure for worry is prayer.

—WILLIAM JAMES

Anxiety is often a red light on the mind's dashboard that tells us we are not expressing our needs to God and trusting his providence.

—RICHARD F. LOVELACE

Nine-tenths of our unhappiness is selfishness and is an insult cast in the face of God.

—G. H. MORRISON

The beginning of anxiety is the end of faith. The beginning of true faith is the end of anxiety.

—GEORGE MUELLER

All worry is atheism, because it is a want of trust in God.

—FULTON SHEEN

Beware of anxiety. Next to sin, there is nothing that so troubles the mind, strains the heart, distresses the soul and confuses the judgment.

—WILLIAM F. ULLATHORNE

Worrying is praying to the wrong God.

—UNKNOWN

Despair is the one sin that cannot be forgiven.

—NGUGI WA THIONG'O

THE BIBLE & BIBLE READING ∼

We must be on guard against giving interpretations of scripture that are far-fetched or opposed to science, and so exposing the word of God to the ridicule of unbelievers.

—ST. AUGUSTINE

Not man's word about God, but God's word about man.

—KARL BARTH

We must read the Bible through the eyes of shipwrecked people for whom everything has gone overboard.

—KARL BARTH

Sink the Bible to the bottom of the ocean, and man's obligations to God would be unchanged. He would have the same path to tread, only his lamp and his guide would be gone; he would have the same voyage to make, only his compass and chart would be overboard.

—HENRY WARD BEECHER

Apply yourself wholly to the text; apply the text wholly to yourself.

—JOHN ALBRECHT BENGEL

Holy Scripture containeth all things necessary to salvation.

—*BOOK OF COMMON PRAYER*

In the twentieth century our highest praise is to call the Bible "the world's best-seller." And it has come to be more and more difficult to say whether we think it is a best-seller because it is great, or vice versa.

—DANIEL BOORSTIN

The Bible sheds a lot of light on the commentaries.

—JOHNNY CASH

God was more exciting then than he is now.

—CHILD'S COMMENT ON THE OLD TESTAMENT

I have spent a lot of time searching through the Bible looking for loopholes.

—W. C. FIELDS, ATTRIBUTED DURING HIS LAST ILLNESS

The Bible should be taught so early and so thoroughly that it sinks straight to the bottom of the mind where everything that comes along can settle on it.

—NORTHROP FRYE

Anyone who reads the Bible and isn't puzzled at least half the time doesn't have his mind on what he's doing.

—GILBERT HIGHET

When you read God's word, you must constantly be saying to yourself, "It is talking to me, and about me."

—SØREN KIERKEGAARD

In short, the Word of God is always contrary to us. When we are self-assured and confident, the word of the law destroys our self-righteousness; when we are depressed and anxious, the word of the gospel declares us righteous.

—CARTER LINDBERG

The Bible was written for men with a head upon their shoulders.

—MARTIN LUTHER

I never saw a useful Christian who was not a student of the Bible. If a person neglects the Bible there is not much for the Holy Spirit to work with. We must have the Word.

—D. L. MOODY

A thorough knowledge of the Bible is worth more than a college education.

—THEODORE ROOSEVELT

The devil can cite Scripture for his purpose.

—WILLIAM SHAKESPEARE,
THE MERCHANT OF VENICE

Defend the Bible? I would just as soon defend a lion. Just turn the Bible loose. It will defend itself.

—CHARLES HADDON SPURGEON

Nobody ever outgrows Scripture; the book widens and deepens with our years.

—CHARLES HADDON SPURGEON

Most people are bothered by those passages in scripture which they cannot understand; but as for me I always noticed that the passages in scripture which trouble me most are those which I do understand.

—MARK TWAIN

If we would destroy the Christian religion, we must first of all destroy man's belief in the Bible.

—VOLTAIRE

I am distressed that our princes take the Word of God no more seriously than a cow does a game of chess.

—ARGULA VON GRUMBACH, SIXTEENTH CENTURY

It is impossible to rightly govern the world without God and the Bible.

—GEORGE WASHINGTON

The Bible is for the government of the people, by the people, and for the people.

—JOHN WYCLIFFE,
IN THE PREFACE TO HIS 1384 TRANSLATION

BUSYNESS ～

O Lord, thou knowest how busy I must be this day; if I forget thee, do not thou forget me: for Christ's sake.

—GENERAL JACOB ASTLEY,
BEFORE THE BATTLE OF EDGEHILL, 1642

The trouble is that I'm in a hurry, but God isn't.

—PHILLIP BROOKS

Hurry is the death of prayer.

—SAMUEL CHADWICK

[God] is always whispering to us, only we do not always hear, because of the noise, hurry and distraction which life causes as it rushes on.

—FREDERICK WILLIAM FABER

There is more to life than increasing its speed.

—MAHATMA GANDHI

Busyness is not of the devil; busyness *is* the devil.

—CARL JUNG

It has been well said that no man ever sank under the burden of the day. It is when tomorrow's burden is added to the burden of today that the weight is more than a man can bear. Never load yourselves so. . . . If you find yourselves so loaded, at least remember this: it is your own doing, not God's. He begs you to leave the future to him, and mind the present.

—GEORGE MacDONALD

Busyness is the enemy of spirituality. It is essentially laziness. It is doing the easy thing instead of the hard thing. It is filling our time with our own actions instead of paying attention to God's actions. It is taking charge.

—EUGENE PETERSON

Everybody else is noisier than God.

—EUGENE PETERSON

[Jesus] was never in a hurry, never impressed by numbers, never a slave of the clock. He was acting, he said, as he observed God to act—never in a hurry.

—J. B. PHILLIPS

God never imposes a duty without giving time to do it.

—JOHN RUSKIN

Remember that it was God who decided on a twenty-four-hour day, and he must have felt that it was enough. We can never do all that we expect ourselves to do, and we can rarely do all that others expect us to do, but we can always do all that God expects us to do.

—SCOTT SERNAU

Busyness is not a synonym for kingdom work—it is only busyness. All activities need to be assessed as to their spiritual authenticity. Again, if we have one hundred things to do and can only do ten, how do we select from among them? We must have God-authored criteria with which to judge our activities, and we must be willing to use them.

—RICHARD A. SWENSON

Do you think Jesus would have carried a pocket calendar? Would he have consulted it before making commitments? Would he have bypassed the leper because his calendar said he was late for the Nazareth spring banquet? . . . The clock and the Christ are not close friends. Imagine what God thinks of us now that we are so locked into schedules that we have locked ourselves out of the Sermon on the Mount—it is hardly possible to walk the second mile today without offending one's pocket calendar. We jump at the alarm of a Seiko but sleep through the call of the Almighty.

—RICHARD A. SWENSON

It is not enough to be busy; so are the ants. The question is: what are we busy about?

—HENRY DAVID THOREAU

On every level of life from housework to heights of prayer, in all judgment and all efforts to get things done, hurry and impatience are sure marks of the amateur.

—EVELYN UNDERHILL

If you're too busy to pray, you're too busy.

—UNKNOWN

Noise and words and frenzied, hectic schedules dull our senses, closing our ears to his still, small voice and making us numb to his touch.

—UNKNOWN

Though I am always in haste, I am never in a hurry because I never undertake more work than I can go through with calmness of spirit.

—JOHN WESLEY

CHRISTIANITY &
THE CHRISTIAN LIFE ∼

Christianity began by insisting that the most diverse people should live together and by enabling them to do so, because they were all living with Jesus.

—WILLIAM BARCLAY

Christianity is unquestionably a personal experience. It is equally unquestionably not a private experience.

—WILLIAM BARCLAY

The essential fact of Christianity is that God thought all men worth the sacrifice of his son.

—WILLIAM BARCLAY

It is not well for a man to pray cream and live skim milk.

—HENRY WARD BEECHER

Faith and works should travel side by side, step answering to step, like the legs of men walking. First faith, and then works; and then faith again, and then works again—until you can scarcely distinguish which is the one and which is the other.

—WILLIAM BOOTH

God promises a safe landing but not a calm passage.

—BULGARIAN PROVERB

It must be admitted that a life is properly formed when and only when it is yielded to God.

—JOHN CALVIN

Christianity, above all, has given a clear-cut answer to the demands of the human soul.

—ALEXIS CARREL

We should live our lives as though Christ was coming this afternoon.

—JIMMY CARTER

The Christian ideal has not been tried and found wanting. It has been found difficult; and left untried.

—G. K. CHESTERTON

Christianity is the land of beginning again.

—W. A. CRISWELL

Christianity is not for the well meaning, but for the desperate.

—JAMES DENNY

The entrance fee to the kingdom of heaven is nothing, the annual subscription is everything.

—HENRY DRUMMOND

The witness of a godly life is never in vain.

—A. S. GILFILLAN

Being a Christian is more than just an instantaneous conversion—it is a daily process whereby you grow to be more and more like Christ.

—BILLY GRAHAM

It is unnatural for Christianity to be popular.

—BILLY GRAHAM

Becoming a Christian must be seen as and believed to be a passing from darkness to light, from death to life—not the joining of a rather pleasant religious club.

—GEORGE G. HUNTER, III

Christianity is good news, not good advice.

—WILLIAM R. INGE

Christianity promises to make men free; it never promises to make them independent.

—WILLIAM R. INGE

The glory of God is a person fully alive.

—IRENAEUS

To know and to serve God, of course, it's why we're here, a clear truth that—like the nose on your face—is near at hand and easily discernible but can make you dizzy if you try to focus on it hard. But a little faith will see you through. What else will do except faith in such a cynical, corrupt time? When the country goes temporarily to the dogs, cats must learn to be circumspect, walk on fences, sleep in trees, and have faith that all this woofing is not the last word.

—GARRISON KEILLOR

Most people really believe that the Christian commandments (e.g., to love one's neighbor as oneself) are intentionally a little too severe—like putting the clock ahead half an hour to make sure of not being late in the morning.

—Søren Kierkegaard

Christianity is not a system of morals, it is the worship of a person.

—W. H. Lecky

I believe in Christianity as I believe in the sun—not only because I see it, but because by it I see everything else.

—C. S. Lewis

Collapse in the Christian life is seldom a blowout; it is usually a slow leak.

—Paul Little

Any serious study of the Christian claim is, at its essence, a study of the cross. . . . Being religious without knowing the cross is like owning a Mercedes with no motor. Pretty package, but where is your power?

—Max Lucado

Christianity taught men that love is worth more than intelligence.

—Jacques Maritain

There are only two kinds of religion in the world. . . . They all say "Do, do, do." Only Christianity says, "Done." Christ has done it all.

—Vernon McGee

The heathen brings a sacrifice to his god; the Christian accepts the sacrifice from his God.

—Henrietta C. Mears

In all your journey as a believer, you will have two categories of spiritual experiences. One is tender, delightful, and loving. The other can be quite obscure, dry, dark, and desolate. God gives us the first one to gain us; he gives us the second to purify us.

—MICHAEL MOLINOS

Christianity is different from all other religions. They are the story of man's search for God. The gospel is the story of God's search for man.

—DEWI MORGAN

Your theology is what you are when the talking stops and the action starts.

—COLIN MORRIS

Christianity is one beggar telling another beggar where he found bread.

—D. T. NILES

No Christian is an only child.

—EUGENE PETERSON

Authentic spirituality is lived in community.

—GORDON T. SMITH

Going to church doesn't make anybody a Christian, any more than taking a wheelbarrow into a garage makes it an automobile.

—BILLY SUNDAY

A man following Christ's teaching is like a man carrying a lantern before him at the end of a pole. The light is ever before him, and ever impels him to follow it, by continually lighting up fresh ground and attracting him onward.

—LEO TOLSTOY

Christianity, with its doctrines of humility, of forgiveness, of love, is incompatible with the State, with its haughtiness, its violence, its punishment, its wars.

—LEO TOLSTOY

If your Christianity won't work where you are, it won't work anywhere.

—UNKNOWN

The doctrine of the kingdom of heaven, which was the main teaching of Jesus, is certainly one of the most revolutionary doctrines that ever stirred and changed human thought.

—H. G. WELLS

Christianity can be condensed into four words: admit, submit, commit, and transmit.

—SAMUEL WILBERFORCE

See also Christians; Discipleship and Commitment

CHRISTIANS ∼

It is not what men eat, but what they digest that makes
   them strong;
Not what we gain, but what we save that makes us rich;
Not what we read, but what we remember that makes
   us learned;
Not what we preach or pray, but what we practice and
   believe that makes us Christians.

—FRANCIS BACON

It is said that a saint is one who always chooses the better of the two courses open to him at every step.

—ROBERT H. BENSON

Christian: One who believes that the New Testament is a divinely inspired book admirably suited to the spiritual needs of his neighbor.

—AMBROSE BIERCE

A saint is one who exaggerates what the world neglects.

—G. K. CHESTERTON

If you were arrested for being a Christian, would there be enough evidence to convict you?

—DAVID OTIS FULLER

A real Christian is a person who can give his pet parrot to a town gossip.

—BILLY GRAHAM

A saint is one who makes it easy to believe in Jesus.

—RUTH BELL GRAHAM

God creates out of nothing. Wonderful, you say. Yes, to be sure, but he does what is still more wonderful: he makes saints out of sinners.

—SØREN KIERKEGAARD

We are not Christians because we do good works; we do good works because we are Christians.

—MARTIN LUTHER

For the wonderful thing about saints is that they were human. They lost their tempers, got angry, scolded God, were egotistical or testy or impatient in their turns, made mistakes and regretted them. Still they went on doggedly blundering toward heaven.

—PHYLLIS MCGINLEY

The Christian is one who has forever given up the hope of being able to think of himself as a good man.

—LESSLIE NEWBIGIN

If Christians wish us to believe in their redeemer, why don't they look a little more redeemed?

—FRIEDRICH NIETZSCHE

The true Christian is in all countries a pilgrim and a stranger.

—GEORGE SANTAYANA

A good Christian is a velvet-covered brick.

—FRED SMITH

The saints are the sinners who keep on trying.

—ROBERT LOUIS STEVENSON

A man becomes a Christian, he is not born one.

—TERTULLIAN

See how these Christians love one another.

—TERTULLIAN

The Christian believes that he was created to know, love and serve God in this world and to be happy with him in the next. That is the sole reason for his existence.

—EVELYN WAUGH

Christians are like tea bags. You never know what kind you are until you are in hot water.

—ELEANOR SEARLE WHITNEY

See also Christianity and the Christian Life

CHRISTMAS ∾

Christmas is [Christ's] monogram, stenciled on our hearts, recalling to us year by year that "no more is God a stranger."

—CHARLES L. ALLEN AND CHARLES L. WALLIS

Christmas is not a date. It is a state of mind.

—MARY ELLEN CHASE

How many observe Christ's birthday! How few, his precepts. O! Tis easier to keep holidays than commandments.

—BENJAMIN FRANKLIN

Christmas has two Ss in it, and they're both $$ signs.

—STAN FREBERG

I sometimes think we expect too much of Christmas Day. We try to crowd into it the long arrears of kindliness and humanity of the whole year.

—DAVID GRAYSON

Next to a circus there ain't nothing that packs up and tears out of town any quicker than the Christmas spirit.

—FRANK MCKINNEY HUBBARD

Our trouble is that we want the peace without the Prince.

—ADDISON H. LEITCH

The Christmas assurance supremely is that God has not forgotten human need.

—CLELAND B. MCAFEE

There were only a few shepherds at the first Bethlehem. The ox and the ass understood more of the first Christmas than the high priests in Jerusalem. And it is the same today.

—Thomas Merton

To perceive Christmas through its wrapping becomes more difficult with every year.

—E. B. White

Santa Claus never died for anybody.

—Craig Wilson

THE CHURCH

I have no objections to churches so long as they do not interfere with God's work.

—Brooks Atkinson

He cannot have God for his father who refuses to have the church for his mother.

—St. Augustine

The Christian church is not exactly known for setting trends or embracing change.

—George Barna

A church needs poor men and wicked men as much as it needs pure men and virtuous men and pious men.

—Henry Ward Beecher

The church is not a gallery for the exhibition of eminent Christians, but a school for the education of imperfect ones.

—Henry Ward Beecher

The continuous and widespread fragmentation of the church has been the scandal of the ages. It has been Satan's master strategy. The sin of disunity probably has caused more souls to be lost than all other sins combined.

—PAUL BILLHEIMER

A congregation who can't afford to pay a clergyman enough want a missionary more than they do a clergyman.

—JOSH BILLINGS

The church is only the church when she exists for others.

—DIETRICH BONHOEFFER

The empty tomb proves the value of Christianity; the empty church denies it.

—DENNY BRAKE

People are driven from the church not so much by stern truth that makes them uneasy, as by weak nothings that make them contemptuous.

—GEORGE BUTTRICK

The hippopotamus's day
Is passed in sleep; at night he hunts;
God moves in a mysterious way—
The church can sleep and feed at once.

—T. S. ELIOT

The church is an anvil that has worn out many hammers.

—ENGLISH PROVERB

Once a church which possessed no paid ministry, no priesthood, no cathedrals or church buildings, no endowments, no salaried bishops or secretaries, and no publicity except lies told by its enemies, held a disintegrating world together and laid the basis of a new civilization. Its power was not its own.

—HAROLD FEY

He who is near the church is often far from God.

—FRENCH PROVERB

Many come to bring their clothes to church rather than themselves.

—THOMAS FULLER

The miracle is that the divine nature of the church is not altogether obscured by the all too human nature of her members.

—WALTER MARSHALL HORTON

Nearly all churches state verbally their desire to grow. Often, however, their profession means "we want to grow if persons will conform to the traditions and values of the church, but we do not want to grow if it requires change."

—BEN JOHNSON

God never intended his church to be a refrigerator in which to preserve perishable piety. He intended it to be an incubator in which to hatch converts.

—F. LINCICOME

The church always arrives on the scene a little breathless and a little late.

—BERNARD J. F. LONERGAN

We tell our Lord plainly that if he will have his church then he must look to and maintain and defend it, for we can neither uphold nor protect it; and if we could, then we should become the proudest asses under heaven.

—MARTIN LUTHER

He wanted life in men, energy, impulse; and in his church he has often found nothing but a certain tame decorum, of which even he can make little.

—W. M. MacGregor

The living church, though never neat, keeps God's world from complete disaster.

—George F. MacLeod

Church: The gin-shop in which men stupefy themselves against the weight of the world's woes.

—Karl Marx

The mystery of the church consists in the very fact that *together* sinners become *something different* from what they are as individuals; this "something different" is the Body of Christ.

—J. Meyendorff

There are many who stay away from church these days because you hardly ever mention God any more.

—Arthur Miller,
The Crucible

The task of organized religion is not to prove that God was in the first century, but that he is in the 20th.

—S. H. Miller

The Christian church is a society of sinners. It is the only society in the world, membership in which is based upon the single qualification that the candidate shall be unworthy of membership.

—Charles Clayton Morrison

The church must be relevant and stop answering questions that no one is asking.

—T. CECIL MYERS

God told me that my church was not growing bigger, it was simply growing fatter.

—JUAN CARLOS ORTIZ

The world does not take the church seriously because the church is not serious. The world is suing us for divorce because of non-support.

—PAUL CALVIN PAYNE

The church has lower standards for membership than those for getting on a bus.

—HARRY R. RUDIN

A place where we must on no account enjoy ourselves and where ladies are trained in the English art of sitting in rows for hours, dumb, expressionless, and with elbows turned in.

—GEORGE BERNARD SHAW

The problem is not that churches are filled with empty pews, but that the pews are filled with empty people.

—CHARLIE SHEDD

Who is forced to go to church will not pray.

—SLOVENIAN PROVERB

The church after all is not a club of saints; it is a hospital for sinners.

—GEORGE STEWART

I believe in the church, one holy, catholic and apostolic, and regret that it nowhere exists.

—WILLIAM TEMPLE

The church is the only organization on earth which does not exist for the sake of its members.

—WILLIAM TEMPLE

The church is a society of sinners, the only organization in the world where one of the conditions of membership is that you must admit you are imperfect. There is no room in the church for the man who feels he is perfect.

—CHARLES B. TEMPLETON

The long experience of the church is more likely to lead to correct answers than is the experience of the lone individual.

—ELTON TRUEBLOOD

Beware when you take on the church of God. Others have tried and bitten the dust.

—DESMOND TUTU

If you don't go to God's house, why should he go to yours?

—UNKNOWN

If you find the perfect church, don't join it—you'll ruin it.

—UNKNOWN

The Bible knows nothing of solitary religion.

—UNKNOWN

The church has many critics but no rivals.

—UNKNOWN

In general the churches, visited by me too often on weekdays . . . bore for me the same relation to God that billboards did to Coca-Cola: they promoted thirst without quenching it.

—JOHN UPDIKE,
A MONTH OF SUNDAYS

Have you ever found God in church? I never did. I just found a bunch of folks hoping for him to show. Any God I ever felt in church I brought in with me. And I think all the other folks did too. They come to church to *share* God, not find God.

—ALICE WALKER

They stopped me from swinging in church, so I had to swing outside.

—FATS WALLER

The church, like the Ark of Noah, is worth saving, not for the sake of the unclean beasts and vermin that almost filled it, and probably made most noise and clamor in it, but for the little corner of rationality that was as much distressed by the stink within as by the tempest without.

—WILLIAM WARBURTON

The aim of God in history is the creation of an all-inclusive community of loving persons, with himself included in that community as its prime sustainer and most glorious inhabitant.

—DALLAS WILLARD

CONFESSION ∾

We have left undone those things which we ought to have done; and we have done those things which we ought not to have done.

—*BOOK OF COMMON PRAYER*

To confess your sins to God is not to tell him anything he doesn't already know. Until you confess them, however, they are the abyss between you. When you confess them, they become the bridge.

—FREDERICK BUECHNER

There may be exceptions but I believe the old rule is a good one—the circle of confession should be as wide as the circle of commission. If I have sinned privately, I confess to God; if I have sinned against an individual, I confess to the individual; if I have sinned publicly, then I confess to the group.

—LEIGHTON FORD

We only confess our little faults to persuade people that we have no big ones.

—FRANÇOIS, DUC DE LA ROCHEFOUCAULD

It's a good start if you feel wretched in God's presence.

—MARTIN LLOYD-JONES

For a good confession three things are necessary: an examination of conscience, sorrow and a determination to avoid sin.

—ST. ALPHONSUS LUGUORI

To admit our sin is positively the most cheerful thing any of us can do.

—UNKNOWN

See also Repentance; Sin and Sinners

DEATH

See in what peace a Christian can die.

—JOSEPH ADDISON,
LAST WORDS

It is dangerous to abandon one's self to the luxury of grief; it deprives one of courage and even of the wish for recovery.

—H. F. AMIEL

Death is the supreme festival on the road to freedom.

—DIETRICH BONHOEFFER

In the midst of life we are in death.

—*BOOK OF COMMON PRAYER*

One short sleep past, we wake eternally,
And Death shall be no more: Death, thou shalt die!

—JOHN DONNE

I must not think it strange that God takes in youth those
whom I would have kept on earth until they were older. God
is peopling eternity, and I must not restrict him to old men
and women.

—JIM ELLIOT

In the last analysis, it is our conception of death which decides
our answers to all the questions that life puts to us.

—DAG HAMMARSKJÖLD

Death for the Christian is a turning off the light because the
dawn has come.

—LEON JAWORSKI

A man is blessed if he is able to keep the hour of his death
continually before his eyes, and every day to hold himself in
readiness for death.

—THOMAS À KEMPIS

Always be ready; always live in such a way that death can
never find you unprepared.

—THOMAS À KEMPIS

Teach me to live, that I may dread
My grave as little as my bed.

—THOMAS KEN

If you knew what he knows about death you would clap your listless hands.

—GEORGE MACDONALD

I acquiesce in my death with complete willingness, uncolored by hesitation; how foolish to cling to life when God has ordained otherwise!

—JORGE MANRIQUE

Death is not a threat to genuine life. It is but a paper tiger that is no longer free to terrorize us once we know the truth about the outcome of the cross. Death is but a temporary inconvenience that separates our smaller living from our greater being.

—CALVIN MILLER

The creative action of the Christian's life is to prepare his death in Christ.

—FLANNERY O' CONNOR

No man ever repented of being a Christian on his deathbed.

—BOB PHILLIPS

Death cannot sever what the cross unites.

—UNKNOWN

See also Suffering and Hardships

DISCIPLESHIP & COMMITMENT ～

Christians are living in this sinful world and must bear its burdens; they may not steal away from the battlefield.

—NICHOLAS BERDYAEV

When Christ calls a man he bids him come and die.

—DIETRICH BONHOEFFER

When Jesus put the little child in the midst of his disciples, he did not tell the little child to become like his disciples, he told the disciples to become like the little child.

—RUTH BELL GRAHAM

Let each remember that he will make progress in all spiritual things only insofar as he rids himself of self-love, self-will and self-interest.

—ST. IGNATIUS OF LOYOLA

[T]here are no shortcuts, no gimmicks, no easy ways to cultivate an intimacy with God and attain the resulting passion that should carry one through life's journey.

—GORDON MACDONALD

Jesus promised his disciples three things: that they would be completely fearless, absurdly happy and in constant trouble.

—F. R. MALTBY

To take up the cross of Christ is no great action done once for all; it consists in the continual practice of small duties which are distasteful to us.

—JOHN HENRY NEWMAN

No pain, no palm; no thorns, no throne; no gall, no glory; no cross, no crown.

—WILLIAM PENN

Spiritual life does not go with a secure life. You have to take risk to save yourself.

—IGNAZIO SILONE, *BREAD AND WINE*

Spiritual growth most likely takes place in a context of routine and discipline.

—GORDON T. SMITH

To be crucified means, first, the man on the cross is facing only one direction; second, he is not going back; and third, he has no further plans of his own.

—A. W. TOZER

No Christian escapes a taste of the wilderness on the way to the Promised Land.

—EVELYN UNDERHILL

If we were willing to learn the meaning of real discipleship and actually to become disciples, the church in the West would be transformed, and the resultant impact on society would be staggering.

—DAVID WATSON

See also Christianity and the Christian Life; Christians

DOUBTS

Doubt is not the enemy of faith, but its constant companion. The great biblical models of faith all had doubts about God's goodness. These doubts never betrayed a lack of faith. Actually, these men and women's faith in God's goodness was so strong that it had to take seriously the questions that seriously challenged God's character. . . . Faith is the prize of those who pass through deep waters and strain for a deeper understanding of their God.

—M. CRAIG BARNES

Doubts are the ants in the pants of faith. They keep it awake and moving.

—FREDERICK BUECHNER

Faith which does not doubt is dead faith.

—MIGUEL DE UNAMUNO

Never doubt in the dark what God told you in the light.

—V. RAYMOND EDMAN

When we are in doubt, God will never fail to give light when we have no other plan than to please him and to act in love for him.

—BROTHER LAWRENCE

Ten thousand difficulties do not make one doubt.

—JOHN HENRY NEWMAN

Doubt is part of all religion. All the religious thinkers were doubters.

—ISAAC BASHEVIS SINGER

There lies more faith in honest doubt, believe me, than in half the creeds.

—ALFRED, LORD TENNYSON

See also Faith; Guidance

EASTER ∼

The heathen, too, believe that Christ died; the belief, the faith in his resurrection makes the Christian Christian. . . . It is faith in this resurrection that justifies us.

—ST. AUGUSTINE

The Easter message tells us that our enemies, sin, the curse, and death, are beaten. Ultimately they can no longer start mischief. They still behave as though the game were not decided, the battle not fought; we must still reckon with them, but fundamentally we must cease to fear them any more.

—KARL BARTH

This is the most important issue you will ever have to decide. Did Jesus rise from the dead or not?

—MICHAEL GREEN

"If you don't believe in Easter," Owen Meany said, "don't kid yourself—don't call yourself a Christian."

—JOHN IRVING,
A PRAYER FOR OWEN MEANY

Easter is to our faith what water is to the ocean, what stone is to the mountain, what blood is to your body.

—RAYMOND I. LINDQUIST

Easter morning is not a mere declaration that we are immortal, but a declaration that we are *immortal children of God.*

—GEORGE MATHESON

The sure knowledge that "Christ has died, Christ is risen, Christ will come again" is so contagious that it can hardly be stifled by the clumsiest of organizations, the most taciturn of members, the most inarticulate of pastors.

—ROY M. OSWALD AND SPEED B. LEAS

Jesus tasted death. But hell's party was cancelled after only three days.

—JOSEPH STOWELL

The simplest meaning of Easter is that we are living in a world in which God has the last word.

—UNKNOWN

The gospels do not explain the resurrection; the resurrection explains the gospels. Belief in the resurrection is not an appendage to the Christian faith, it *is* the Christian faith.

—JOHN S. WHALE

EVANGELISM ～

Evangelism is simply telling the good news of what God has done for us and the whole world in the life, death and resurrection of Jesus Christ in the confident expectation that God will move and act among our hearers in his own way and time.

—DONALD BLOESCH

It is a form of trade, you see. I ask God for souls and pay him by giving up everything else.

—ST. JOHN BOSCO

To convert the poor, you must be like them; to convert the rich, you must be unlike them.

—DOROTHY DAY

You can win more converts with a spoonful of honey than a barrelful of vinegar.

—ST. FRANCIS DE SALES

How many prodigals are kept out of the kingdom of God by the unlovely characters of those who profess to be inside.

—HENRY DRUMMOND

Kindness has converted more sinners than zeal, eloquence or learning.

—FREDERICK WILLIAM FABER

Evangelism is not complete until the evangelized become the evangelists.

—BILLY GRAHAM

Nobody will believe you have a new life unless they see a new lifestyle. And when they see it, they'll be ready to listen about the new life—and not before.

—MICHAEL GREEN

The most potent evangelism is that which takes place daily, weekly, yearly through the work of the local church.

—GEORGIA HARKNESS

The problem today is that the spiritual situation is desperate, but many of God's people are not.

—VANCE HAVNER

Evangelism does not primarily aim at reform, education, cultural development or human betterment, necessary as these are. They are the by-products of evangelism after a person is established in a proper relationship with God through Christ.

—HOWARD KEELEY

The main business of a Christian soul is to go through the world turning its water into wine.

—ANDREW LANG

The minister lives behind a "stained glass curtain." The layman has opportunities for evangelism which a minister will never have.

—JAMES I. MCCORD

It is more effective to spend time talking to Christ about a man than talking to a man about Christ, because if you are talking to Christ about a man earnestly, trustingly, in the course of time you cannot help talking to the man effectively about Christ.

—ROBERT BOYD MUNGER

It is as absurd to argue men, as to torture them, into believing.

—JOHN HENRY NEWMAN

[A]ll structures are a hindrance to people in their search for God. If people have to accept Christ plus the pipe organ, the piano, the program and the television ministry, millions will reject Christ. The more things we add to Christ, the more things people have to accept with Christ, the more difficult it is for them to respond.

—JUAN CARLOS ORTIZ

The trouble with witnessing for Christ in the world is that it is at times almost impossible not to antagonize the rich, the well-established, the ruling classes, and important people within the church itself.

—ALAN PATON

These early Christians (in the book of Acts) were led by the Spirit to the main task of bringing people to God through Christ, and were not permitted to enjoy fascinating sidetracks.

—J. B. PHILLIPS

Christians and non-Christians have something in common: we're both uptight about evangelism.

—REBECCA PIPPERT

In the Great Commission the Lord has called us to be, like Peter, fishers of men. We've turned the commission around so that we have become merely keepers of the aquarium. Occasionally I take some fish out of your fishbowl and put them into mine, and you do the same with my bowl. But we're all tending the same fish.

—SAM SHOEMAKER

Most people are brought to faith in Christ not by argument for it but by exposure to it.

—SAM SHOEMAKER

Evangelism is the normal life of the church and can never be an optional extra.

—JOHN STOTT

Some want to live within the sound of church or chapel bell; I want to run a rescue shop within a yard of hell.

—C. T. STUDD

One is Christianized to the extent that he is a Christianizer. One is evangelized to the extent that he is an evangelist.

—LEO JOZEF SUENENS

Our task as laymen is to live our personal communion with Christ with such intensity as to make it contagious.

—PAUL TOURNIER

It is not enough to give a cup of cold water; it is necessary also to tell why.

—ELTON TRUEBLOOD

You are a Christian today because somebody cared. Now it's your turn.

—WARREN W. WIERSBE

It is the temptation of this pragmatic age to presume that technique is the secret of evangelism.

—A. SKEVINGTON WOOD, 1956

See also Mission

EVIL ∾

Evil: That which God does not will.

—EMIL BRUNNER

Evil is whatever dehumanizes. Humanness is the realization of love, self-awareness, empathy towards others, inner peace, ecstatic joy and a host of other fruits of the Spirit. Whenever personal relationships, vocational activities, play and religious life develop these qualities in us, there is good. And whenever [they] diminish our humanness, there is evil. God is at work through the former. Satan is at work in the latter.

—TONY CAMPOLO

Evil is the destruction of God's creation. It is an unmaking of his form and order. God starts with nothing and moves through chaos to greater and greater design. Evil goes the opposite direction. It takes order and turns it back to chaos and eventually wants the nothing again—the death wish come true.

—JOHN CLAYPOOL

Evil deeds are like perfume—difficult to hide.

—GHANAIAN PROVERB

Never open the door to a lesser evil, for other and greater ones invariably slink in after it.

—BALTASAR GRACIAN

Evil is not human; it is the defect and opposite of the human; but the suffering that follows it is human, belonging of necessity to the human that has sinned. . . .

—GEORGE MACDONALD

Blessed is he who has it in his power to do evil, yet does it not.

—MARGUERITE OF NAVARRE

One of the dangers of focusing on evil is that you can lose your bearings. Perhaps the mystery of human evil isn't as great or magnificent as the extraordinary mystery of human goodness.

—M. SCOTT PECK

The moment we permit evil to control our imaginations, dictate the way we think, and shape our responses, we at the same time become incapable of seeing the good and the true and the beautiful.

—EUGENE PETERSON

As surely as God is good, so surely there is no such thing as necessary evil.

—ROBERT SOUTHEY

Evil is the quiet acceptance of that which we know to be wrong. Noncooperation with evil is a Christian duty.

—JIM WALLIS

See also Satan; Sin and Sinners

FAITH ～

I do not seek to understand that I may believe, but I believe that I may understand. For this too I believe, that unless I first believe I shall not understand.
—ST. ANSELM

Faith is believing what one cannot see, and the reward of faith is to see what one believes.
—ST. AUGUSTINE

God never goes back on the man who stakes his all on him.
—WILLIAM BARCLAY

Faith is never identical with piety.
—KARL BARTH

Faith is not a thing one "loses," we merely cease to shape our lives by it.
—GEORGES BERNANOS

You can do very little with faith but you can do nothing without it.
—NICHOLAS M. BUTLER

Faith in antagonism to common sense is fanaticism, and common sense in antagonism to faith is rationalism. The life of faith brings the two into a right relation.

—OSWALD CHAMBERS

When people cease to believe in God, they don't believe in nothing; they believe in everything.

—G. K. CHESTERTON

Whatever happens, abide steadfast in a determination to cling simply to God.
—ST. FRANCIS DE SALES

All I have seen teaches me to trust the Creator for all I have not seen.

—RALPH WALDO EMERSON

If the work of God could be comprehended by reason, it would no longer be wonderful, and faith would have no merit if reason provided proof.

—POPE GREGORY I

Faith in God will not get for you everything you may want, but it will get for you what God wants you to have. The unbeliever does not need what he wants: the Christian should want only what he needs.

—VANCE HAVNER

Where there is the necessary technical skill to move mountains, there is no need for the faith that moves mountains.

—ERIC HOFFER

Faith begins as an experiment and ends as an experience.

—WILLIAM R. INGE

We think we believe, but is our faith really awake, or is it lying bed-ridden in some dormitory of our souls?

—WILLIAM R. INGE

It is so hard to believe because it is so hard to obey.

—SØREN KIERKEGAARD

Man is capable of nothing; it is God who gives everything, who gives man faith.

—SØREN KIERKEGAARD

Faith is the belief that God is real and that God is good. Faith is not a mystical experience or a midnight vision or a voice in the forest . . . it is a choice to believe that the one who made it all hasn't left it all and that he still sends light into shadows and responds to the gestures of faith.

—MAX LUCADO

What greater rebellion, impiety, or insult to God can there be, than not to believe his promises.

—MARTIN LUTHER

You never test the resources of God until you attempt the impossible.

—F. B. MEYER

Faith embraces many truths which seem to contradict each other.

—BLAISE PASCAL

If you can't believe in God the chances are your God is too small.

—J. B. PHILLIPS

To believe means to recognize that we must wait until the veil shall be removed. Unbelief prematurely unveils itself.

—EUGEN ROSENSTOCK-HUESSY

It is at night that faith in light is admirable.

—EDMOND ROSTAND

Faith means giving as much of myself as I know to as much of Christ as I know.

—SAM SHOEMAKER

Two signposts of faith: Slow Down and Wait Here.

—CHARLES STANLEY

Faith is not shelter against difficulties but belief in the face of all contradictions.

—PAUL TOURNIER

Faith is not belief without proof, but trust without reservation.

—ELTON TRUEBLOOD

When Jesus healed the man blind from birth, he let him grope his way, still blind, to wash in the pool—and *then* the light broke. We don't need to know what we're groping toward—or why. It is enough that we have Christ's direction. The light will break in God's own time.

—UNKNOWN

You know that if you get in the water and have nothing to hold on to, but try to behave as you would on dry land, you will drown. But if, on the other hand, you trust yourself to the water and let go, you will float. And this is exactly the situation of faith.

—ALAN WATTS

The kind of faith God values seems to develop best when everything fuzzes over, when God stays silent, when the fog rolls in.

—PHILIP YANCEY

See also Doubts; Guidance; Hope

FEAR ~

Fear only two: God, and the man who has no fear of God.

—HASIDIC SAYING

I said to a man who stood at the gate of the year: "Give me a light that I may tread safely into the unknown." And he replied, "Go out into the darkness and put your hand into the hand of God. That shall be to you better than a light and safer than a known way."

—MINNIE L. HASKINS

There is a virtuous fear which is the effect of faith, and a vicious fear which is the product of doubt and mistrust. The former leads to hope as relying on God, in whom we believe; the latter inclines to despair. . . . Persons of the one character fear to lose God; those of the other character fear to find him.

—BLAISE PASCAL

O Christ, who hast known fear, be with all who are afraid today.

—UNITED SOCIETY FOR THE PROPAGATION
OF THE GOSPEL

Fear: the tax that conscience pays to guilt.

—UNKNOWN

Three fears weaken the heart: fear of the truth, fear of poverty, and fear of the devil.

—WELSH PROVERB

FORGIVENESS ⁓

He who forgives ends the quarrel.

—AFRICAN PROVERB

There is one eternal principle which will be valid as long as the world lasts. The principle is: forgiveness is a costly thing. . . . And God alone can pay the terrible price that is necessary before men can be forgiven. Forgiveness is never a case of saying, "It's all right, it doesn't matter." Forgiveness is the most costly thing in the world.

—WILLIAM BARCLAY

"I can forgive, but I cannot forget," is only another way of saying "I cannot forgive."

—HENRY WARD BEECHER

It is easier to forgive an enemy than to forgive a friend.

—WILLIAM BLAKE

The glory of Christianity is to conquer by forgiveness.

—WILLIAM BLAKE

Forgiveness is man's deepest need and God's highest achievement.

—HORACE BUSHNELL

Where is the foolish person who would think it is in his power to commit more than God could forgive?

—ST. FRANCIS DE SALES

Forgive, son; men are men, they needs must err.

—EURIPIDES

The weak can never forgive. Forgiveness is the attribute of the strong.

—MAHATMA GANDHI

If his conditions are met, God is bound by his Word to forgive any man or any woman of any sin because of Christ.

—BILLY GRAHAM

Forgiveness is the answer to the child's dream of a miracle by which what is broken is made whole again, what is soiled is again made clean.

—DAG HAMMARSKJÖLD

He that cannot forgive others breaks the bridge over which he must pass himself; for every man has need to be forgiven.

—GEORGE HERBERT

If you forgive people enough you belong to them, and they to you, whether either person likes it or not—squatter's rights of the heart.

—JAMES HILTON

A wise man will make haste to forgive, because he knows the true value of time.

—SAMUEL JOHNSON

To err is human, to forgive divine.

—ALEXANDER POPE

We should forgive in verbs, not in nouns. Forgive people for what they *do*, not for what they *are*. Retail forgiving is for us, not wholesale. It is hard enough to forgive anyone for doing a bad thing; it is almost impossible to forgive someone for being a bad person. Not even God forgives us for what we are. He forgives us for what we do and then accepts us for what we are.

—LEWIS SMEDES

No other system, ideology or religion proclaims a free forgiveness and a new life to those who have done nothing to deserve it but deserve judgment instead.

—JOHN STOTT

The fully forgiven man does not rejoice in his own forgiveness but in the divine love to which he owes it; and his past sin persists in his experience no longer as a source of shame but as the occasion of a new wonder in his adoration of the love divine.

—WILLIAM TEMPLE

Only one petition in the Lord's prayer has any condition attached to it: it is the petition for forgiveness.

—WILLIAM TEMPLE

When God forgives he forgets. He buries our sins in the sea and puts up a sign on the bank saying, "No fishing allowed."

—CORRIE TEN BOOM

Forgiveness is the fragrance that the flower leaves on the heel of the one who crushed it.

—MARK TWAIN

Men with clenched fists cannot shake hands.

—UNKNOWN

When you forgive, you in no way change the past, but you sure do change the future.

—UNKNOWN

There is so much for all of us to forgive that we shall never get it done without putting in a lot of practice.

—J. NEVILLE WARD

GOD ⁓

What is impossible to God? Not that which is difficult to his power, but that which is contrary to his nature.

—St. Ambrose

God is an infinite circle whose center is everywhere and whose circumference is nowhere.

—St. Augustine

As I grow older, I care less and less what people think about me and more and more what God thinks of me. I expect to be with him much longer than with you.

—Robert Baker

Man can certainly flee from God . . . but he cannot escape him. He can certainly hate God and be hateful to God, but he cannot change into its opposite the eternal love of God which triumphs even in his hate.

—Karl Barth

To believe in God is to know that all the rules will be fair and that there will be wonderful surprises.

—Ugo Betti

God educates peoples as he educates individuals, by putting them in tight places.

—Salem G. Bland

A God who would let us prove his existence would be an idol.

—Dietrich Bonhoeffer

God is weak and powerless in the world, and that is precisely the way, the only way, in which he is with us and helps us. . . . Only the suffering God can help.

—Dietrich Bonhoeffer

It is as impossible for man to demonstrate the existence of God as it would be for even Sherlock Holmes to demonstrate the existence of Arthur Conan Doyle.

—Frederick Buechner

Although Satan does his part, God still retains supreme authority.

—John Calvin

A comprehended God is no God.

—John Chrysostom

God moves in a mysterious way
His wonders to perform;
He plants his footsteps in the sea,
And rides upon the storm.

—William Cowper

We always keep God waiting while we admit more importunate suitors.

—Malcolm de Chazal

What God does he does well.

—Jean de la Fontaine

These people who want to tell God how to run the universe, they remind me of those people with five shares in some corporation who take up the entire stockholders' meeting telling the directors how to run their business.

—Peter de Vries,
The Blood of the Lamb

As he that fears God fears nothing else, so, he that sees God sees everything else.

—John Donne

Suppose a man is hiding and he stirs, he shows his where-
abouts. . . . God does the same. No one could ever have found
God; he gives himself away.

—MEISTER ECKHART

God does not play dice with the world.

—ALBERT EINSTEIN

I heard from a hillbilly revivalist that God is the croupier, and
never loses.

—MARTIN FISCHER

I could prove God statistically. Take the human body alone—
the chances that all the functions of an individual would just
happen is a statistical monstrosity.

—GEORGE H. GALLUP

Let us fear God and we shall cease to fear man.

—MAHATMA GANDHI

Art is a collaboration between God and the artist, and the less
the artist does the better.

—ANDRÉ GIDE

I have never understood why it should be considered deroga-
tory to the creator to suppose that he has a sense of humor.

—WILLIAM R. INGE

He who leaves God out of his reckoning does not know how
to count.

—ITALIAN PROVERB

What God does not choose to give, you cannot take.

—JEWISH SAYING

The remarkable thing about the way in which people talk about God, or about their relation to God, is that it seems to escape them completely that God hears what they are saying.

—Søren Kierkegaard

A man with God is always in the majority.

—John Knox

[Y]ou can safely assume you've created God in your own image when it turns out that God hates all the same people you do.

—Anne Lamott

The finger of God never leaves identical fingerprints.

—Stanislaus Lec

Jehovah does not think or behave like a social worker.

—Doris Lessing

My great concern is not whether God is on our side, my great concern is to be on God's side.

—Abraham Lincoln

Dear God: Are you really invisible or is that just a trick?

—Lucy, in *Children's Letters to God*

I must continually remind myself as I lecture: if God is God then it is ridiculous to talk about him as if he is not present.

—Lesslie Newbigin

What matters supremely, therefore, is not . . . the fact that I know God, but the larger fact which underlies it—the fact that *he knows me*.

—J. I. Packer

The knowledge of God is very far from the love of him.

—BLAISE PASCAL

God is up to something so big, so unimaginably good that your mind cannot contain it. . . . What we see God doing is never as good as what we don't see.

—BEN PATTERSON

The Bible isn't interested in whether we believe in God or not. It assumes that everyone more or less does. What it is interested in is the response we have toward him.

—EUGENE PETERSON

[God] cannot change for the better, for he is already perfect; and being perfect, he cannot change for the worse.

—A. W. PINK

Ever since the days of Adam, man has been hiding from God and saying, "God is hard to find."

—FULTON SHEEN

Don't feel totally, personally, irrevocably responsible for everything; that's my job—God.

—SIGN ON A PASTOR'S DESK

Our love of God is tested by the question of whether we seek him or his gifts.

—RALPH W. SOCKMAN

Too many are waiting for God to do something for them rather than with them.

—RALPH W. SOCKMAN

The best proof of God's existence is what follows when we deny it.

—WILLIAM L. SULLIVAN

Do not have your concert first and tune your instruments afterward. Begin the day with God.

—JAMES HUDSON TAYLOR

To be right with God has often meant to be in trouble with men.

—A. W. TOZER

God does not ask much of a man but he asks all of him that there is.

—UNKNOWN

God does not invest a man with power from on high for any other work than that of his kingdom.

—UNKNOWN

Humor is God's aspirin.

—UNKNOWN

When God measures a man, he puts the tape around the heart instead of the head.

—UNKNOWN

If God created us in his own image we have more than reciprocated.

—VOLTAIRE

In the opinion that there is a God, there are difficulties; but in the contrary opinion there are absurdities.

—VOLTAIRE

Isn't it the greatest possible disaster, when you are wrestling with God, not to be beaten.

—SIMONE WEIL

What is the chief end of man?
To glorify God and to enjoy him forever.

—THE WESTMINSTER CATECHISM

Although God is good, this does not mean he is goody-goody, or that all he does is pleasant and agreeable to human tastes.

—VICTOR WHITE

Don't bargain with God.

—YIDDISH PROVERB

If God lived on earth, people would break his windows.

—YIDDISH PROVERB

GOD'S PROVISION ~

If I am faithful to the duties of the present, God will provide for the future.

—GREGORY T. BEDELL

God's gifts put man's best dreams to shame.

—ELIZABETH BARRETT BROWNING

God gives every bird its food, but he does not throw it into the nest.

—JOSIAH G. HOLLAND

Dear God: I know you will provide, but why don't you provide *until* you provide?

—JEWISH SAYING

If a man is admitted into the bullion vault of a bank, and told to help himself, and comes out with one cent, whose fault is it that he is poor? Whose fault is it that Christian people generally have such scanty portions of the free riches of God?

—ALEXANDER MACLAREN

He who gives us teeth will give us bread.

—YIDDISH PROVERB

See also Grace

GOD'S WILL ∽

God of all goodness, grant us to desire ardently, to seek wisely, to know surely and to accomplish perfectly thy holy will, for the glory of thy name.
—THOMAS AQUINAS

All heaven is waiting to help those who will discover the will of God and do it.
—J. ROBERT ASHCROFT

The strength of a man consists in finding out the way in which God is going, and going that way too.
—HENRY WARD BEECHER

In his will is our peace.
—DANTE

Wanting what God wants is the only learning that can give us peace of mind.
—FRANÇOIS DE MALHERBE

People of ordinary goodness walk in God's way, but the devout run in it, and at length they almost fly therein. To be truly devout, we must not only do God's will, but we must do it cheerfully.
—ST. FRANCIS DE SALES

There are no disappointments to those whose wills are buried in the will of God.
—FREDERICK WILLIAM FABER

A knowledge of the will of God is relative to one's desire to do the will of God. God does not reveal his will to those who are not gladly committed to it. A commission from God is relative to our commitment to God.

—DON W. HILLIS

My Father, teach us not only thy will, but how to do it. Teach us the best way of doing the best thing, lest we spoil the end by unworthy means.

—J. H. JOWETT

Man proposes but God disposes.

—THOMAS À KEMPIS

There is always time enough in a day to do God's will.

—ROY LESSIN

My God, give me neither poverty nor riches, but whatsoever it may be Thy will to give, give me with it a heart that knows humbly to acquiesce in what is Thy will.

—GOTTHOLD EPHRAIM LESSING

There are only two kinds of people in the end: those who say to God, "Thy will be done," and those to whom God says, "*Thy* will be done."

—C. S. LEWIS

I am satisfied that when the Almighty wants me to do or not to do any particular thing, he finds a way of letting me know it.

—ABRAHAM LINCOLN

If it is God's will that I must die at the hand of an assassin, I must be resigned. I must do my duty as I see it, and leave the rest with God.

—ABRAHAM LINCOLN

Has it ever struck you that the vast majority of the will of God for your life has already been revealed in the Bible? That is a crucial thing to grasp.

—PAUL LITTLE

I am immortal until the will of God for me is accomplished.

—DAVID LIVINGSTONE

God has a way of frustrating our personal goals until they are reorganized with his kingdom at the center.

—RICHARD F. LOVELACE

Blessed is he who submits to the will of God; he can never be unhappy.

—MARTIN LUTHER

Doing the will of God leaves me no time for disputing his plans.

—GEORGE MACDONALD

Feed upon the will of God and drink the chalice of Jesus with your eyes shut, so that you may not see what is inside.

—ST. PAUL OF THE CROSS

Most people don't want to know the will of God in order to do it; they seem to want to know it just in order to consider it!

—WILLIAM L. PETTINGILL

Ascertaining God's will is often a painful and heart-searching experience, mainly because most of us have an inner reluctance to do the will of God without reservation.

—J. OSWALD SANDERS

That which is often asked of God, is not so much his will and way, as his approval of our way.

—SARAH F. SMILEY

The center of God's will is our only safety.

—BETSIE TEN BOOM

The will of God will never lead you where the grace of God cannot keep you.

—UNKNOWN

God shuts one door in order to open a hundred doors.

—YUGOSLAV PROVERB

See also Guidance; Work and Vocation

THE GOSPEL MESSAGE ∼

If you believe what you like in the gospel, and reject what you like, it is not the gospel you believe but yourself.

—ST. AUGUSTINE

Jesus came to raise the dead. The only qualification for the gospel is to be dead. You don't have to be smart. You don't have to be good. You don't have to be wise. You don't have to be wonderful. You don't have to be anything. You just have to be dead. That's it.

—ROBERT CAPON

Most of us read the gospels with sealed and unwondering eyes.

—DEAN CHURCH

To keep the good news to ourselves would be in effect to repudiate its validity.

—ROBERT E. COLEMAN

Preach the gospel at all times. If necessary, use words.

—ST. FRANCIS OF ASSISI

When I use the word "gospel" I'm talking about the power of God to change people so they can live in the world as disciples of Christ, rubbed into all of the social institutions around them.

—RICHARD HALVERSON

There is no such thing as a "personal gospel" or a "social gospel." There is but one gospel . . . and it has two applications, personal and social. Both are necessary; one without the other is incomplete. A purely social gospel is like a body without a soul—it is a corpse. A purely personal gospel is like a soul without a body—it is a ghost.

—E. STANLEY JONES

Dwight L. Moody commented that the gospel is like a lion. All the preacher has to do is to open the door of the cage and get out of the way!

—ROBERT MOUNCE

The music changes, but the message never does.

—DUANE PEDERSON

Gospel, as everyone knows, means tiding, news, good news. Not views, mark you, but news. The substitution of views for news is one of the most damaging and deadening things that can happen to religion. Sometimes the church itself has become infected by the error, and has been so preoccupied with man's view of God that there has been little time or energy left for heralding God's news to man.

—JAMES S. STEWART

You say that you believe the gospel: you live as if you were not sure one word of it is true.

—THOMAS WILSON

See also The Bible and Bible Reading

GRACE ～

The grace of God is outrageous. By normal human reason, it doesn't make any sense.

—LEITH ANDERSON

God loves each of us as if there were only one of us.

—ST. AUGUSTINE

Cheap grace is grace without discipleship, grace without the cross, grace without Jesus Christ, living and incarnate. . . . Costly grace is the treasure hidden in the field; for the sake of it a man will gladly go and sell all that he has. It is costly because it costs a man his life, and it is grace because it gives a man the only true life.

—DIETRICH BONHOEFFER

There, but for the grace of God, goes John Bradford.

—JOHN BRADFORD,
ON SEEING A CRIMINAL PASS BY
(A SENTIMENT ALSO ATTRIBUTED TO OTHERS)

Excessive activism is typical of those who do not live by grace.

—CHARLES BRÜTSCH

Thank God, he does not measure grace out in teaspoons.

—AMY CARMICHAEL

God never gives strength for tomorrow, or for the next hour, but only for the strain of the minute.

—OSWALD CHAMBERS

We are never without help. We have no right to say of any good work, it is too hard for me to do, or of any sorrow, it is too hard for me to bear, or of any sinful habit, it is too hard for me to overcome.

—ELIZABETH CHARLES

None can harm God's proteges.

—GEOFFROI DE VILLEHARDOUIN

How can we ever be the sold short or the cheated, we who for every service have long ago been overpaid.

—MEISTER ECKHART

Grace is but glory begun, and glory is but grace perfected.

—JONATHAN EDWARDS

My mother told me I was blessed, and I have always taken her word for it. Being born of . . . royalty is nothing like being blessed. Royalty is inherited from another human being, blessedness comes from God.

—DUKE ELLINGTON

The doctrines of grace humble a man without degrading him, and exalt a man without inflating him.

—CHARLES HODGE

The word "grace" is unquestionably the most significant single word in the Bible.

—ILION T. JONES

They travel lightly whom God's grace carries.

—THOMAS À KEMPIS

He will never let us go, he will always recall us. His covenant love will always outwit our sinful stupidity any day.

—DENNIS LENNON

It seems to me that we often, almost sulkily, reject the good that God offers us because, at the moment, we expected some other good.

—C. S. Lewis

Grace always gives, whereas sin always takes away.

—Martin Lloyd-Jones

The granting of restorative grace is among the greatest and most unique gifts one Christian can give another.

—Gordon MacDonald

If the good God were suddenly
To make a solitary Blind to see
We would stand wondering all
And call it a miracle;
But that he gives with lavish hand
Sight to a million souls we stand
And say, with little awe,
He but fulfills a natural law.

—Huw Menai

A man can no more take in a supply of grace for the future than he can eat enough for the next six months, or take sufficient air into his lungs at one time to sustain life for a week. We must draw upon God's boundless store of grace from day to day as we need it.

—D. L. Moody

Remember the great need you have of the grace and assistance of God. You should never lose sight of him—not for a moment.

—Andrew Murray

Often the nature of grace can be made plain only by describing its absence.

—Flannery O' Connor

Man is born broken. He lives by mending. And, the grace of God is glue.

—EUGENE O'NEILL,
THE GREAT GOD BROWN

There is no depth to which we can fall that our Lord will not stoop to find us and reclaim us.

—LLOYD OGILVIE

The law imposed what it did not give. Grace gives what it imposes.

—BLAISE PASCAL

A person has to get fed up with the ways of the world before he, before she, acquires an appetite for the world of grace.

—EUGENE PETERSON

He doesn't wait to see how we turn out to decide to choose us or not to choose us.

—EUGENE PETERSON

Without the burden of afflictions it is impossible to reach the height of grace. The gifts of grace increase as the struggles increase.

—ST. ROSE OF LIMA

Our heavenly father is longing to do good things for us. If we aren't experiencing his goodness, it is because we really don't believe it.

—BASILEA SCHLINK

Grace is too unpredictable, too lavish, too delicious for us to stay sober about it. What can you do with such unchecked generosity but smack your lips, slosh it around your tongue, and savor it with joy.

—LEWIS SMEDES

Life can be horrible, horrible beyond enduring, the pits. But the secret of grace is that it can be all right at the center even when it's all wrong on the edges. For at the center where life is open to the Creator and Savior God, we are held, led, loved, cared for and inseparably bound into the future that he has for every child that he claims as his.

—LEWIS SMEDES

The grace of God is in my mind shaped like a key, that comes from time to time and unlocks the heavy doors.

—DONALD SWAN

Some of his choicest deliveries come through the back door of our lives.

—CHARLES SWINDOLL

Accept the fact that you are accepted.

—PAUL TILLICH

Grace is the good pleasure of God that inclines him to bestow benefits upon the undeserving.

—A. W. TOZER

God interferes in the lives of men and women, seeking to start them on the road to salvation.

—COLIN WILLIAMS

GRATITUDE ⁓

No duty is more urgent than that of returning thanks.

—ST. AMBROSE

Gratitude is not only the dominant note in Christian piety, but equally the dominant motive of Christian action in the world. Such gratitude is for the grace that has been shown to us. . . .

—JOHN BAILLIE

How worthy it is to remember former benefits when we come
to beg for new.

—STEPHEN CHARNOCK

The most important prayer in the world is just two words
long: "Thank you."

—MEISTER ECKHART

O Thou who hast given us so much, mercifully grant us one
more thing—a grateful heart.

—GEORGE HERBERT

To stand on one leg and prove God's existence is a very different thing from going down on one's knees and thanking him.

—SØREN KIERKEGAARD

Gratitude is not a virtue that comes easy to the human race.

—W. SOMERSET MAUGHAM

Gratitude takes nothing for granted, is never unresponsive, is
constantly awakening to new wonder, and to praise of the
goodness of God.

—THOMAS MERTON

You have to celebrate your chosenness constantly. This means
saying "thank you" to God for having chosen you, and "thank
you" to all who remind you of your chosenness. Gratitude is
the most fruitful way of deepening your consciousness that
you are not an "accident," but a divine choice.

—HENRI NOUWEN

It must be an odd feeling to be thankful to nobody in particular. Christians in public institutions often see this odd thing happening on Thanksgiving Day. Everyone in the institution seems to be "thankful in general." It's very strange. It's a little like being married in general.

—CORNELIUS PLANTINGA

The worst moment for the atheist is when he is really thankful, and has nobody to thank.

—CHRISTINA ROSSETTI

The beginning of men's rebellion against God was, and is, the lack of a thankful heart.

—FRANCIS SCHAEFFER

I think it pisses God off if you walk by the color purple in a field somewhere and don't notice it.

—ALICE WALKER

GUIDANCE ～

God is the God of abundance. There are twelve baskets full of pieces of bread left over. In life's decisions, God doesn't always bring us into places where all choices are between right and wrong. In his greatness, his children often find themselves in the enviable position of choosing among two or more rights! It would have been right to take any one of the pieces of bread that Christ multiplied.

—JAY ADAMS

The place God calls you to is the place where your deep gladness and the world's deep hunger meet.

—FREDERICK BUECHNER

The history of all the great characters of the Bible is summed up in this one sentence: they acquainted themselves with God, and acquiesced in his will in all things.

—RICHARD CECIL

Not revelation it is that waits, but our unfurnished eyes.

—EMILY DICKINSON

God never closed one gap without opening another.

—IRISH PROVERB

If you are not guided by God you will be guided by someone or something else.

—ERIC LIDDELL

The demand to know where we are going, is one which no Christian has a right to make.

—LESSLIE NEWBIGIN

In our quest for God's guidance we become our own worst enemies, and our mistakes attest to our nuttiness in this area.

—J. I. PACKER

It is impossible to doubt that guidance is a reality intended for, and promised to, every child of God. Christians who miss it thereby show only that they did not seek it as they should. It is right therefore to be concerned about one's own receptiveness to guidance, to study how to seek it.

—J. I. PACKER

Men give advice; God gives guidance.

—LEONARD RAVENHILL

There is nothing so small but that we may honor God by asking his guidance of it, or insult him by taking it into our own hands.

—JOHN RUSKIN

Never dig up in unbelief what you have sown in faith. Begin with the confidence that God will guide and end with the assurance that he has guided.

—J. OSWALD SANDERS

The plain fact is that not everyone who professes to seek guidance is honestly desirous of being guided into God's will.

—J. OSWALD SANDERS

If God gives you a watch, are you honoring him more by asking him what time it is or by simply consulting the watch?

—A. W. TOZER

The man or woman who is wholly or joyously surrendered to Christ can't make a wrong choice—any choice will be the right one.

—A. W. TOZER

Faith accepts quiet guidance. Only unbelief demands a miracle.

—UNKNOWN

God made the moon as well as the sun: and when he does not see fit to grant us the sunlight, he means us to guide our steps as well as we can by moonlight.

—RICHARD WHATELY

You can't hear God speak to someone else, you can hear him only if you are being addressed.

—LUDWIG WITTGENSTEIN

See also Doubts; God's Will; Waiting; Work and Vocation

HEAVEN ～

To believe in heaven is not to run away from life; it is to run toward it.

—JOSEPH D. BLINCO

Heaven is filled with converted sinners of all kinds and there is room for more.

—ST. JOSEPH CAFASSO

Heaven is a cheap purchase, whatever it cost.

—ENGLISH PROVERB

Christians are not citizens of earth trying to get to heaven but citizens of heaven making their way through this world.

—VANCE HAVNER

No man can resolve himself into heaven.

—D. L. MOODY

If I ever reach heaven I expect to find three wonders there: first, to meet some I had not thought to see there; second, to miss some I had expected to see there; and third, the greatest wonder of all, to find myself there.

—JOHN NEWTON

Heaven is the presence of God.

—CHRISTINA ROSSETTI

There are no crown-wearers in heaven that were not cross-bearers here below.

—CHARLES HADDON SPURGEON

Christmas morning for ever and ever.

—UNKNOWN

Heaven is a prepared place for a prepared people, and they that enter shall find that they are neither unknown or unexpected.

—UNKNOWN

See also Hell

HELL ～

Then I saw that there was a way to hell, even from the gates of heaven.

—JOHN BUNYAN

Abandon all hope, you who enter here.

—DANTE

The road to hell is paved with good intentions.

—ENGLISH PROVERB

If there is no belief in hell the concept of judgment also becomes meaningless; and then all that is left of Christianity is a system of ethics.

—GEOFFREY GORER

If we had more hell in the pulpit, we would have less hell in the pew.

—BILLY GRAHAM

Hell is truth seen too late.

—GEORG WILHELM FRIEDRICH HEGEL

The safest road to hell is the gradual one—the gentle slope, soft underfoot, without sudden turnings, without milestones, without signposts.

—C. S. LEWIS

The one principle of hell is, "I am my own!"

—GEORGE MacDONALD

Long is the way
and hard, that out of hell leads up to light.

—JOHN MILTON

It is not always realized that Jesus spoke more often of hell
than of heaven. For him the consequences of unforgiven sin
were terrible to contemplate.

—LEON MORRIS

Nothing burneth in hell but self-will.

—THEOLOGICA GERMANICA

The way down to hell is easy.

—VIRGIL

The damned is no less an inmate of hell because he does not
believe in it.

—FRANZ WERFEL

See also Heaven

HOLINESS ∾

God does not require a perfect, sinless life to have fellowship
with him, but he does require that we be serious about holiness, that we grieve over sin in our lives instead of justifying
it, and that we earnestly pursue holiness as a way of life.

—JERRY BRIDGES

Holiness does not consist in mystic speculations, enthusiastic fervors or uncommanded austerities; it consists in thinking as God thinks and willing as God wills.

—JOHN BROWN

As alien and archaic as the idea may seem the task of the church is not to make men and women happy, it is to make them holy.

—CHARLES W. COLSON

Saying "yes" to God means saying "no" to things which offend his holiness.

—A. MORGAN DERHAM

One of the holiest women I have ever known did little with her life in terms of worldly success; her gift was that of bringing laughter with her, no matter how dark or grievous the occasion. Wherever she was, holy laughter was present to heal and redeem.

—MADELEINE L'ENGLE

The ambition of my life is to be as holy as a saved sinner can be.

—ROBERT MURRAY MCCHEYNE

A holy person is one who is sanctified by the presence and action of God within him.

—THOMAS MERTON

It is a great deal better to live a holy life than to talk about it.

—D. L. MOODY

Holiness is not an optional extra to the process of creation but rather the whole point of it.

—DONALD NICHOLL

[S]tanding in a church singing a hymn doesn't make us holy any more than standing in a barn and neighing makes us a horse.

—EUGENE PETERSON

The greatest miracle that God can perform today is to take an unholy man out of an unholy world, and make that man holy and put him back into that unholy world and keep him holy in it.

—LEONARD RAVENHILL

Holiness consists of doing the will of God with a smile.

—MOTHER TERESA

There is nothing high-minded about Christian holiness. It is most at home in the slum, the street, the hospital ward.

—EVELYN UNDERHILL

Holiness is living that pleases God.

—UNKNOWN

Remember the weekday to keep it holy.

—UNKNOWN

There is such a thing as the danger of a selfish pursuit of holiness.

—GERALD VANN

In our age, as in every age, people are longing for happiness, not realizing that what they are looking for is holiness.

—JERRY L. WALLS

Associate with sanctified persons; they may, by their counsel, prayers and holy example, be a means to make you holy.

—THOMAS WATSON

[H]oliness is not optional for the Christian. It is not an elective. It is your major.

—JOHN WHITE

HOLY SPIRIT ✑

God is love; God is fire. The two are one. The Holy Spirit baptizes with fire. Spirit-filled souls are ablaze for God. They love with a love that glows.

—SAMUEL CHADWICK

Sometimes the wisest tactic is to get out of the Holy Spirit's way.

—JUDITH COUCHMAN

Nor shall I believe that you are in the Spirit except I behold in you the fruits of the Spirit.

—ERASMUS

Those who have the gale of the Holy Spirit go forward even in sleep.

—BROTHER LAWRENCE

God commands us to be filled with the Spirit; and if we aren't filled, it's because we're living beneath our privileges.

—D. L. MOODY

Every time we say, "I believe in the Holy Spirit," we mean that we believe that there is a living God able and willing to enter human personality and change it.

—J. B. PHILLIPS

The outstanding characteristics of twentieth century Christianity . . . are impotence and ineffectiveness in witness. The reason . . . is not hard to trace. In both pulpit and pew there tends to be a practical ignoring of the Holy Spirit who mediates the power of the risen Christ.

—J. OSWALD SANDERS

The true believer in the Holy Spirit is one who knows how to hoist the sail of his own spirit to catch the winds of God.

—RALPH W. SOCKMAN

[W]hen things are at their worst, you had better be alert and wakeful, more vigilant then than ever, for that is the likeliest hour for a new decisive emergence of the Spirit of God upon the scene.

—JAMES S. STEWART

Without the work of the Spirit in our hearts, even Jesus is a great unknown.

—JAMES S. STEWART

Before Christ sent the church into world he sent the Spirit into the church. The same order must be observed today.

—JOHN STOTT

I have a glove here in my hand. The glove cannot do anything by itself, but when my hand is in it, it can do many things. True, it is not the glove, but my hand in the glove that acts. We are gloves. It is the Holy Spirit in us who is the hand, who does the job. We have to make room for the hand so that every finger is filled.

—CORRIE TEN BOOM

The idea of the Spirit held by the average church members is so vague as to be nearly nonexistent.

—A. W. TOZER

The Pharisees looked straight at the Light of the World for three years, but not one ray of light reached their inner beings. Light is not enough. The inward operation of the Holy Spirit is necessary to saving faith. The gospel is light but only the Spirit can give sight.

—A. W. TOZER

Holy Wind
Blow across my mind,
Free me
Of the things that bind.

—UNKNOWN

A simple definition of the Holy Spirit is "God in action today."

—ALAN WALKER

HOME, FAMILY, & MARRIAGE

O Creator, who does all human beings make, thou has a great worth on us conferred by bringing us this little child.

—AFRICAN PRAYER

The religion of a child depends on what its mother and father are, and not on what they say.

—H. F. AMIEL

Those whom God has joined together let no man put asunder.

—*BOOK OF COMMON PRAYER*

Every Christian family ought to be, as it were, a little church, consecrated to Christ, and wholly influenced and governed by his rules.

—JONATHAN EDWARDS

Keep your eyes open before marriage, half shut afterwards.

—BENJAMIN FRANKLIN

The most important thing a father can do for his children is to love their mother.

—THEODORE HESBURGH

In most cases, an unhappy single person will be an unhappy married person. A bitter, angry single person will be a bitter, angry married person. . . . Marriage does not produce life or character transformations. Such changes are produced by the inner work of the Holy Spirit which is not dependent on one's marital status.

—BILL AND LYNNE HYBELS

The woman who creates and sustains a home, and under whose hands children grow up to be strong and pure men and women is a creator second only to God.

—HELEN HUNT JACKSON

God could not be everywhere and therefore he made mothers.

—JEWISH PROVERB

It is easier for a father to have children than for children to have a real father.

—POPE JOHN XXIII

No man is poor who has had a godly mother.

—ABRAHAM LINCOLN

There is no more lovely, friendly and charming relationship, communion or company than a good marriage.

—MARTIN LUTHER

No matter how many communes anybody invents, the family always creeps back.

—MARGARET MEAD

A baby is God's opinion that the world should go on.

—CARL SANDBURG

An ounce of mother is worth a pound of clergy.

—Spanish proverb

When home is ruled according to God's Word, angels might be asked to stay with us, and they would not find themselves out of their element.

—Charles Haddon Spurgeon

Two processes ought never to be entered prematurely: embalming and divorce.

—Charles Swindoll

The goal of our life should not be to find joy in marriage, but to bring more love and truth into the world. We marry to assist each other in this task. The most selfish and hateful life of all is that of two beings who unite in order to enjoy life. The highest calling is that of the man who has dedicated his life to serving God and doing good, and who unites with a woman in order to further that purpose.

—Leo Tolstoy

When a father complains that his son has taken to evil ways, what should he do? Love him more than ever.

—Israel Baal Shem Tov

History teaches us that there is no substitute for the family if we are to have a society that stands for human beings at their best.

—Ray Lyman Wilbur

See also Love; Relationships

HOME, FAMILY, & MARRIAGE

HOPE ～

When you say a situation or a person is hopeless, you are slamming the door in the face of God.

—CHARLES L. ALLEN

Everything that is done in the world is done by hope. No husbandman would sow one grain of corn if he hoped not it would grow up and become seed; no bachelor would marry a wife if he hoped not to have children; no merchant or tradesman would set himself to work if he did not hope to reap benefit thereby.

—MARTIN LUTHER

Hope springs eternal in the human breast.

—ALEXANDER POPE

It is impossible for that man to despair who remembers that his helper is omnipotent.

—JEREMY TAYLOR

Hope is faith holding out its hand in the dark.

—UNKNOWN

Hope is putting faith to work when doubting would be easier.

—UNKNOWN

In all things it is better to hope than to despair.

—JOHANN WOLFGANG VON GOETHE

See also Faith

HUMILITY ∾

The greater you are, the more you must practice humility.

—THE APOCRYPHA

If you are looking for an example of humility, look at the cross.

—THOMAS AQUINAS

It is no great thing to be humble when you are brought low; but to be humble when you are praised is a great and rare achievement.

—BERNARD OF CLAIRVAUX

The true way to be humble is not to stoop until you are smaller than yourself, but to stand at your real height against some higher nature that will show you what the real smallness of your greatness is.

—PHILLIP BROOKS

Always remember that there are two types of people in this world. Those who come into a room and say, "Well, here I am!" and those who come in and say, "Ah, there you are!"

—FREDERICK L. COLLINS

It is difficult to be humble. Even if you aim at humility, there is no guarantee that when you have attained the state you will not be proud of the feat.

—BONAMY DOBRÉE

Nothing sets a person so much out of the devil's reach as humility.

—JONATHAN EDWARDS

Humility is the most difficult of all virtues to achieve; nothing dies harder than the desire to think well of oneself.

—T. S. ELIOT

Be not angry that you cannot make others as you wish them to be since you cannot make yourself as you wish yourself to be.

—THOMAS À KEMPIS

Moses spent forty years thinking he was somebody; then he spent forty years on the back side of the desert realizing he was nobody; finally, he spent the last forty years learning what God can do with a nobody.

—D. L. MOODY

Humble people don't think less of themselves . . . they just think about themselves less.

—NORMAN VINCENT PEALE

The call to humility is a call to serve God with sober minds—with full awareness of our gifts and our limitations.

—GORDON T. SMITH

Humility is the proper estimate of oneself.

—CHARLES HADDON SPURGEON

Humility is nothing but the truth. Humility is a synonym for honesty, not hypocrisy. It is not an artificial pretense about myself, but an accurate assessment of myself.

—JOHN STOTT

Be humble, that you may not be humbled.

—THE TALMUD

There is no room for God in a person who is full of himself.

—ISRAEL BAAL SHEM TOV

Too humble is half proud.

—YIDDISH PROVERB

THE INTELLECT ∼

Love clings to Christ even when the intellect cannot understand.

—WILLIAM BARCLAY

God cannot be grasped by the mind. If he could be grasped he would not be God.

—EVAGRIUS OF PONTUS

I do not feel obliged to believe that the same God who has endowed us with sense, reason and intellect has intended us to forgo their use.

—GALILEO

For some reason many people today think that having a good theological foundation is nothing more than academic and intellectual elitism when the simplest Puritan plowman would have been expected to have a basic theological knowledge.

—OS GUINNESS

If someone had told me I would be Pope one day, I would have studied harder.

—POPE JOHN PAUL I

God guides through your heightened moral intelligence. "Can you not of yourselves judge that which is right?" said Jesus. He expected us to think our way to right Christian conclusions.

—E. STANLEY JONES

Even God has been defended with nonsense.

—WALTER LIPPMANN

It is the heart that experiences God, not the reason.

—BLAISE PASCAL

It does not take a great mind to be a Christian but it takes all the mind a man has.

—RICHARD C. RAINES

Nowhere does [Jesus] demand of his hearers that they shall sacrifice thinking to believing.

—ALBERT SCHWEITZER

We are in the most anti-intellectual period in the history of the church. People don't want to hear that stuff. They want to be entertained. They want the quick and easy answer.

—R. C. SPROUL

Wisdom is the right use of knowledge. To know is not to be wise. Many men know a great deal, are all the greater fools for it. . . . But to know how to use knowledge is to have wisdom.

—CHARLES HADDON SPURGEON

He came to take away your sins, not your mind.

UNKNOWN

We must ask people to think, but we should not expect them to become theologians before they are Christians.

—UNKNOWN

Christians must realize that just as a fire cannot burn without fuel, so burning hearts are not kindled by brainless heads. We must not be content to have zeal without knowledge.

—DONALD WHITNEY

JESUS ∼

He became what we are that he might make us what he is.

—ATHANASIUS

Our glory must always be not in what we can do for Christ but in what Christ can do for us.

—WILLIAM BARCLAY

Hold to Christ, and for the rest be totally uncommitted.

—HERBERT BUTTERFIELD

If Jesus Christ were to come today, people would not even crucify him. They would ask him to dinner, and hear what he had to say, and make fun of it.

—THOMAS CARLYLE

Today we often tend to treat the Lord Jesus something like a convenience food—handy to have around in case of an unexpected need.

—MARGARET CLARKSON

In darkness there is no choice. It is light that enables us to see the difference between things: and it is Christ that gives us light.

—J. C. AND A. W. HARE

Christ either deceived mankind by conscious fraud, or he was himself deluded, or he was divine. There is no getting away from this trilemma.

—A. M. HUNTER

If every person in the world had adequate food, housing, income; if all men were equal; if every possible social evil and injustice were done away with, men would still need one thing: Christ!

—J. W. HYDE

I am a candidate for conversion. Bring me something better than Jesus and his way, and I'll take it.

—E. STANLEY JONES

Religion is falling in love with God; and it is impossible to fall in love with an abstract God. He must have a name. . . . The Christian faith says boldly to mankind, "Come, let us introduce you to God. His name is Jesus, and he was a carpenter by trade."

—G. A. STUDDERT KENNEDY

We're more popular than Jesus now; I don't know which will go first—rock 'n' roll or Christianity.

—JOHN LENNON,
OF THE BEATLES, 1966

Either this man was, and is, the Son of God: or else a madman or something worse. But don't let us come with any patronizing nonsense about his being a great human teacher. He hasn't left that open to us. He didn't intend to.

—C. S. LEWIS

What are we to make of Christ? This is a question which has, in a sense, a frantically comic side. For the real question is not what we are to make of Christ, but what is he to make of us. The picture of a fly sitting deciding what it is going to make of an elephant has comic elements about it.

—C. S. LEWIS

If you try to imitate Christ the world will praise you; if you become Christlike it will hate you.

—MARTIN LLOYD-JONES

I know men and I tell you that Jesus Christ is no mere man. Between him and every other person in the world there is no possible term of comparison. Alexander, Caesar, Charlemagne and I have founded empires. But upon what did we rest the creation of our genius? Upon force. Jesus Christ founded his empire upon love, and at this hour millions of men would die for him.

—NAPOLEON

Jesus is the rosetta stone in the language of love.

—NORAH JANE PIGMAN

The whole of history is incomprehensible without him.

—ERNEST RENAN

What other people think of me is becoming less and less important; what they think of Jesus because of me is critical.

—CLIFF RICHARD, BRITISH POP STAR

The New Testament never simply says "remember Jesus Christ." That is a half-finished sentence. It says "remember Jesus Christ is risen from the dead."

—ROBERT RUNCIE

The people who hanged Christ never, to do them justice, accused him of being a bore—on the contrary, they thought him too dynamic to be safe. It has been left for later generations to muffle up that shattering personality and surround him with an atmosphere of tedium. We have very efficiently pared the claws of the Lion of Judah, certified him "meek and mild," and recommended him as a fitting household pet for pale curates and pious old ladies.

—DOROTHY SAYERS

No one would have been invited to dinner as often as Jesus was unless he was interesting and had a sense of humor.

—CHARLES M. SCHULTZ

"Gentle Jesus, meek and mild" is a snivelling modern invention, with no warrant in the gospels.

—GEORGE BERNARD SHAW

I have a great need for Christ; I have a great Christ for my need.

—CHARLES HADDON SPURGEON

You will never know that Jesus is all you need until Jesus is all you've got.

—MOTHER TERESA

If Christ as Lord is the center of our lives, the circumference will take care of itself.

—UNKNOWN

Christ is more of an artist than the artists; he works in the living Spirit and the living flesh; he makes *men* instead of statues.

—VINCENT VAN GOGH

Jesus loves me—this I know,
For the Bible tells me so.

—SUSAN WARNER

We do not need Christ to tell us that the world is full of trouble. But we do need his explanation of history if its troubles are not to be meaningless.

—MICHAEL WILCOCK

If he had never lived, we would not have been able to invent him.

—WALTER WINK

I have one passion, it is he, he alone.

—COUNT ZINZENDORF

JOY ∼

Joy is really the simplest form of gratitude.

—KARL BARTH

The test of Christian character should be that a man is a joy-bearing agent to the world.

—HENRY WARD BEECHER

There is not one blade of grass, there is no color in this world that is not intended to make us rejoice.

—JOHN CALVIN

Joy is the gigantic secret of the Christian.

—G. K. CHESTERTON

God is enjoying himself and he expects us to join him.

—MEISTER ECKHART

As the hand is made for holding and the eye for seeing, thou has fashioned me for joy. Share with me the vision that shall find it everywhere: in the wild violet's beauty; in the lark's melody; in the face of a steadfast man; in a child's smile; in a mother's love; in the purity of Jesus.

—GAELIC PRAYER

When I think of God, my heart is so filled with joy that the notes fly off as from a spindle.

—FRANZ JOSEPH HAYDN,
WHEN CRITICIZED FOR THE JOYFULNESS OF HIS MUSIC

If we are silent about the joy that comes from knowing Jesus, the very stones will cry out! For we are an Easter people and "Alleluia" is our song.

—POPE JOHN PAUL II

We see God as a celestial Scrooge who leans down over the balcony of heaven trying to find anybody who's enjoying life, and says: "Now, cut it out!"

—PAUL LITTLE

Joy is the echo of God's life in us.

—JOSEPH MARMION

Deacon Sims comes down the aisle,
I wish Deacon Sims would smile.
Deacon Sims looks slightly bored —
Not like one who loves the Lord.

—LOIS GRANT PALCHES

The surest mark of a Christian is not faith, or even love, but joy.

—SAM SHOEMAKER

Joy is the standard that flies on the battlements of the heart when the King is in residence.

—R. LEONARD SMALL

Joy is the surest sign of the presence of God.

—PIERRE TEILHARD DE CHARDIN

One filled with joy preaches without preaching.

—MOTHER TERESA

This is the secret of joy. We shall no longer strive for our own way; but commit ourselves, easily and simply, to God's way, acquiesce in his will and in so doing find our peace.

—EVELYN UNDERHILL

Life need not be easy to be joyful. Joy is not the absence of trouble but the presence of Christ.

—WILLIAM VANDER HOVEN

Be merry, really merry. The life of a true Christian should be a perpetual jubilee, a prelude to the festivals of eternity.

—ST. THEOPHANE VENARD

The opposite of joy is not sorrow. It is unbelief.

—LESLIE D. WEATHERHEAD

Sour godliness is the Devil's religion.

—JOHN WESLEY

The Bible is a book of joy. There are 542 references to joy in the Bible. The gospel of salvation in Jesus Christ is a passport to joy. The secret of Jesus was—and is—his inner joy.

—SHERWOOD WIRT

LEADERSHIP ∼

Today we see a massive wholesale and unwitting importation of the worldly principles of leadership into the leadership of the Body of Christ. Many Christian leaders are so success-oriented and power thirsty that they have resorted to dominance over the flock of Christ under their care.

—NDUBUISI B. AKUCHIE

The would-be leader of men who affirms and proclaims that he pays no heed to the things of the Spirit is not worthy to lead them.

—MIGUEL DE UNAMUNO

Let us be servants in order to be leaders.

—FEODOR DOSTOEVSKY

When God creates a leader, he gives him the capacity to make things happen.

—TED ENGSTROM

[I]t is impossible to lead without facing opposition. Progress for God equals resistance from Satan.

—GLENN JOHNSON

One of the greatest ironies of the history of Christianity is that its leaders constantly gave in to the temptation to power—political power, military power, economic power, or moral and spiritual power even though they continued to speak in the name of Jesus, who did not cling to his divine power but emptied himself and became as we are.

—HENRI NOUWEN

The Christian leader of the future is called to be completely irrelevant and to stand in this world with nothing to offer but his or her vulnerable self.

—HENRI NOUWEN

The Christian leader's chief occupational hazards are depression and discouragement.

—JOHN STOTT

A true and safe leader is likely to be one who has no desire to lead, but is forced into a position of leadership by the inward pressure of the Holy Spirit and the press of the external situation.

—A. W. TOZER

The true leader will have no desire to lord it over God's heritage, but will be humble, gentle, self-sacrificing and altogether as ready to follow as to lead, when the Spirit makes it clear that a wiser and more gifted man than himself has appeared.

—A. W. TOZER

A Christian leader who is ambitious to be a star disqualifies himself as a leader.

—DAVID WATSON

LOVE ～

Love has hands to help others. It has feet to hasten to the poor and needy. It has eyes to see misery and want. It has ears to hear the sighs and sorrows of men. This is what love looks like.

—ST. AUGUSTINE

It is much easier to preach the gospel of love for mankind than it is to love single, individual, not very lovable sinners.

—WILLIAM BARCLAY

We like someone *because;* we love someone *although.*

—H. DE MONTHERLANT

We cannot help conforming ourselves to what we love.

—ST. FRANCIS DE SALES

Brotherly love is still the distinguishing badge of every true Christian.

—MATTHEW HENRY

You love God as much as the one you love the least.

—JOHN J. HUGO

Ceasing to be "in love" need not mean ceasing to love.

—C. S. LEWIS

On the whole, God's love for us is a much safer subject to think about than our love for him.

—C. S. LEWIS

The only cure for the love of power is the power of love.

—SHERRI MCADAM

Our job is to love people we don't have to love.

—KEITH MILLER

Love talked about can be easily turned aside but love demonstrated is irresistible.

—W. STANLEY MOONEYHAM

Love without justice is a Christian impossibility, and can only be practiced by those who have divorced religion from life, who dismiss a concern for justice as "politics" and who fear social change much more than they fear God.

—ALAN PATON

People can only be loved into the kingdom.

—J. B. PHILLIPS

Love is essentially the gift of oneself to another.

—MICHEL QUOIST

If we do not show love to one another, the world has a right to question whether Christianity is true.

—FRANCIS SCHAEFFER

Someday, after mastering the winds, the waves, the tides and gravity, we shall harness for God the energies of love, and then, for the second time in the history of the world, man will discover fire.

—PIERRE TEILHARD DE CHARDIN

God doesn't look at how much we do but with how much love we do it.

—MOTHER TERESA

Man's greatest sin is not hatred, but indifference to one's brothers.

—MOTHER TERESA

I am convinced that nine out of ten persons seeing a psychiatrist do not need one. They need somebody who will love them with God's love . . . and they will get well.

—PAUL TOURNIER

The central purpose of Christ's life . . . is to destroy the life of loneliness and to establish here on earth the life of love.

—THOMAS WOLFE

MATERIALISM, MONEY, & POSSESSIONS ∽

If you would know what the Lord God thinks of money, you have only to look at those to whom he gives it.

—MAURICE BARING

Their property held them in chains . . . which shackled their courage and choked their faith and hampered their judgment and throttled their souls . . . if they stored up their treasure in heaven, they would not now have an enemy and a thief within their household . . . enslaved as they are to their own property, they are not the masters of their money, but its slaves.

—ST. CYPRIAN

Jesus talked a great deal about money. Sixteen of the thirty-eight parables were concerned with how to handle money and possessions. In the gospels, an amazing one out of ten verses (288 in all) deal directly with the subject of money. The Bible offers 500 verses on prayer, less than 500 verses on faith, but more than 2,000 verses on money and possessions.

—HOWARD DAYTON, JR.

Share everything with your brother. Do not say, "It is private property." If you share what is everlasting, you should be that much more willing to share things which do not last.

—THE DIDACHE

We are made loveless by our possessions.

—ELIZABETH OF THURINGIA

Things are in the saddle and ride mankind.

—RALPH WALDO EMERSON

Don't forget it: he has much who needs least. Don't create necessities for yourself.

—José Escriva

Learn to enjoy things without owning them.

—Richard Foster

The modern hero is the poor boy who becomes rich rather than the Franciscan or Buddhist ideal of the rich boy who voluntarily becomes poor.

—Richard Foster

Increase of material comforts, it may generally be laid down, does not in any way whatsoever conduce to moral growth.

—Mahatma Gandhi

Property: the more common it becomes the more holy it becomes.

—St. Gertrude

We buy things we do not want to impress people we do not like.

—Arthur Gish

In a consumer society there are inevitably two kinds of slaves: the prisoners of addiction and the prisoners of envy.

—Ivan Illich

Things are to be used and God is to be loved. We get into trouble when we begin to use God and love things.

—Jay Kesler

Cotton Mather commented that piety had begotten prosperity, and the daughter had devoured the mother.

—Richard F. Lovelace

God divided the hand into fingers so that money could slip through.

—MARTIN LUTHER

If our goods are not available to the community, they are stolen goods.

—MARTIN LUTHER

Can we deny that our god and our idol is our standard of living?

—JAMES A. PIKE

Money is one of the acid tests of character and a surprising amount of space is given to it in Scripture. . . . Whether a man is rich or poor, observe his reaction to his possessions and you have a revealing index to his character.

—J. OSWALD SANDERS

Mammon is the largest slaveholder in the world.

—FREDERICK SAUNDERS

Those who set out to serve both God and Mammon soon discover that there is no God.

—LOGAN PEARSALL SMITH

You cannot love money and your brethren at the same time.

—EMMANUEL SUHARD

God is ashamed when the prosperous boast of his special favor.

—RABINDRANATH TAGORE

Nothing that is God's is obtainable by money.

—TERTULLIAN

It doesn't take large quantities of money to come between us and God; just a little, placed in the wrong position, will effectively obscure our view.

—A. W. TOZER

Make all you can, save all you can, give all you can.

—JOHN WESLEY

Material affluence in no respect lessens my need to rely on God. Actually it increases it. I am in greater spiritual danger when I have plenty than when I have nothing. Hence the almost greater need of the wealthy to cry to God for mercy that they may not fail to trust him.

—C. STACEY WOODS

You must leave your possessions behind when God summons.

—YIDDISH PROVERB

MIRACLES ~

We must first make up our minds about Christ before coming to conclusions about the miracles attributed to him.

—F. F. BRUCE

Where there is great love, there are always miracles.

—WILLA CATHER

The most unbelievable thing about miracles is that they happen.

—G. K. CHESTERTON

It is absurd for Christians to constantly seek new demonstrations of God's power, to expect a miraculous answer to every need, from curing ingrown toenails to finding parking spaces; this only leads to faith in miracles instead of faith in God.

—CHARLES W. COLSON

There is in every miracle a silent chiding of the world, and a tacit reprehension of them who require, or who need miracles.

—JOHN DONNE

Cana of Galilee. . . . Ah, that sweet miracle! It was not men's grief, but their joy Christ visited. He worked his first miracle to help men's gladness.

—FEODOR DOSTOEVSKY

All miracles are simply feeble lights like beacons on our way to the port where shines the light, the total light of the resurrection.

—JACQUES ELLUL

There are no miracles to the man who does not believe in them.

—FRENCH PROVERB

Miracles can occur without special effects. It takes more doing for a holy God to forgive an errant person than it does to part the waters of a sea.

—MARTIN MARTY

Jesus was himself the one convincing and permanent miracle.

—IAN MCLAREN

An event which creates faith; that is the purpose and nature of miracles.

—GEORGE BERNARD SHAW

If the world is really the medium of God's personal action, miracle is wholly normal.

—ELTON TRUEBLOOD

By order of the King: "It is forbidden for God to work miracles here."

—UNKNOWN; WRITTEN AT THE ENTRANCE TO A FRENCH
CEMETERY THAT HAD BEEN CLOSED BY KING LOUIS XV
BECAUSE OF SOME MIRACLES THAT WERE SUPPOSEDLY
RESULTING FROM THE RELICS OF SOMEONE BURIED THERE

God performs the impossible; the possible we are required and obligated to do ourselves.

—UNKNOWN

To ask for a miracle in order to believe simply shows there was no intention of believing in the first place.

—UNKNOWN

All is miracle. The stupendous order of nature, the revolution of a hundred millions of worlds, around a million of suns, the activity of light, the life of animals, all are grand and perpetual miracles.

—VOLTAIRE

One must not rely on miracles.

—YIDDISH PROVERB

MISCELLANEOUS ～

The greatness of a man's power is the measure of his surrender.

—WILLIAM BOOTH

My worth to God in public is what I am in private.

—OSWALD CHAMBERS

Love means to love that which is unlovable, or it is no virtue at all; forgiving means to pardon that which is unpardonable, or it is no virtue at all—and to hope means hoping when things are hopeless, or it is no virtue at all.

—G. K. CHESTERTON

Very religious people always shock slightly religious people by their blasphemous attitude to religion and it was precisely for blasphemy that Jesus was crucified.

—R. G. COLLINGWOOD

Men reject their prophets and slay them, but they love their martyrs and honor those whom they have slain.

—FEODOR DOSTOEVSKY

Nature is God's greatest evangelist.

—JONATHAN EDWARDS

We hand folks over to God's mercy, and show none ourselves.

—GEORGE ELIOT

He is no fool, who gives what he cannot keep to gain what he cannot lose.

—JIM ELLIOT

You must live with people to know their problems, and live with God in order to solve them.

—P. T. FORSYTH

Measure not men by Sundays, without regarding what they do all the week after.

—THOMAS FULLER

Wisdom is seeing things from God's perspective.

—BILL GOTHARD

I shall pass through this world but once. Any good thing therefore, that I can do, or any kindness that I can show to any human being, let me do it now. Let me not defer or neglect it, for I shall not pass this way again.

—STEPHEN GRELLET

In some para-church ministries the computer has almost made the Holy Spirit redundant. God could fail to speak to these ministries for ten years and they would run on cheerfully without ever noticing it.

—OS GUINNESS

Why do you hasten to remove anything which hurts your eye, while if something affects your soul you postpone the cure until next year?

—HORACE

God will not look you over for medals, degrees or diplomas, but for scars.

—ELBERT HUBBARD

God likes help when helping people.

—IRISH PROVERB

We cannot love good if we do not hate evil.

—ST. JEROME

When the stomach is full it is easy to talk of fasting.

—ST. JEROME

Be kind, for everyone you meet is fighting a hard battle.

—PHILO JUDAEUS

It is thy duty oftentimes to do what thou wouldst not; thy duty, too, to leave undone what thou wouldst do.

—THOMAS À KEMPIS

When the day of judgement comes, we shall not be asked what we have read, but what we have done, not if we made fine speeches, but if we lived religious lives.

—THOMAS À KEMPIS

The modern theory that you should always treat the religious convictions of other people with profound respect finds no support in the gospels. Mutual tolerance of religious views is the product not of faith, but of doubt.

—ARNOLD LUNN

On the outer fringe of the parish are the four-wheelers—those who come only by pram [stroller] for their christening, taxi for their wedding and hearse for their funeral.

—PERCY LUTTON

It will cost something to be religious: it will cost more to be not so.

—J. MASON

It is an awful condemnation for a man to be brought by God's providence face to face with a great possibility of service and blessing, and then to show himself such that God has to put him aside, and look for other instruments.

—IAN MCLAREN

I was twenty years old before I ever heard a sermon on regeneration. I was always told to be good, but you might as well tell a midget to be a giant as to tell him to be good without telling him how.

—D. L. MOODY

Trust in God but tie your camel.

—PERSIAN PROVERB

One on God's side is a majority.

—Wendell Phillips (also attributed to others)

Religious zeal, if not guarded by God's word, is destructive.

—James Reapsome

It is not by change of circumstances, but by fitting our spirits to the circumstances in which God has placed us, that we can be reconciled to life and duty.

—F. W. Robertson

God often visits us but most of the time we are not at home.

—Joseph Roux

It's a sad commentary when a Christian gets involved in a controversy with a non-Christian and the onlookers can't tell which is which.

—G. Roger Schoenhals

Atheist: a man who has no invisible means of support.

—Fulton Sheen (also attributed to others)

Government laws are needed to give us civil rights, and God is needed to make us civil.

—Ralph W. Sockman

When the hot word of God is poured over a cold, cold world, things break, and it is into this brokenness that we are called . . . with fire in our bones, to show a frightened world that it is not the heat of the fire that we fear, but the chill that lies ahead if the fire goes out.

—Barbara Brown Taylor

You can't change circumstances and you can't change other people, but God can change you.

—Evelyn A. Thiessen

Make sure it's God's trumpet you are blowing—if it is only yours, it won't wake the dead; it will simply disturb the neighbors.

—W. Ian Thomas

It is scarcely possible in most places to get anyone to attend a meeting where the only attraction is God.

—A. W. Tozer

Courage is fear that has said its prayers.

—Unknown

God did not rescue [the Israelites] because they lived a moral life. He called them to live a moral life because he had already rescued them.

—Unknown

People wrap themselves up in the flimsy garments of their own righteousness and then complain of the cold.

—Unknown

What you are is God's gift to you; what you make of it is your gift to God.

—Anthony Dalla Villa
(also attributed to others)

The danger is not lest the soul should doubt whether there is any bread, but lest, by a lie, it should persuade itself that it is not hungry.

—Simone Weil

By night an atheist half believes a God.

—Edward Young

MISSION ～

Mission is not the kindness of the lucky to the unlucky, it is mutual, united obedience to the one God whose mission it is.

—ANGLICAN MANIFESTO, TORONTO, 1963

We are the children of the converts of foreign missionaries; and fairness means that I must do to others as men once did to me.

—MALTBIE D. BABCOCK

A church exists by mission as fire exists by burning.

—EMIL BRUNNER

So far as I know this is the only church [the Moravians] which has ever had more members on the mission fields than it did at home.

—LEIGHTON FORD

If God calls you to be a missionary, don't stoop to be a king.

—JORDON GROOMS

It is a mistake to suppose that a dull and second-rate man is good enough for the heathen. The worst-off need the very best we have. God gave his best, even his only begotten son, in order to redeem a lost world. The most darkened and degraded souls need the best thinking.

—ADONIRAM JUDSON

The needs of the mission field are always far greater than the needs of the church at home, [so] that no human qualifications, however high, render a man or woman more than adequate for missionary work, that there is no other career which affords such scope for enterprise and creative work, and that in comparison with the slight sacrifice demanded, the reward is great beyond all measure.

—STEPHEN NEILL

The church exists for mission. A missionless church is reduced to an activity center for members only. The church of Jesus Christ does serve the wide-ranging needs of her members, but she also mobilizes her members into her savior's mission.

—D. C. POSTERSKI

A difference of opinion is what makes horseraces and missionaries.

—WILL ROGERS

Jesus said that where our treasure is, there our heart will be also. If our spending patterns, then, are an indicator of where our heart is hot and where it is not, at what level would missions register compared to soft drinks?

—JOHN AND SYLVIA RONSVALLE

You are either a missionary or a mission field: one of the two.

—OLAF SKINSNES

I look upon foreign missionaries as the scaffolding around a rising building. The sooner it can be dispensed with, the better; or rather, the sooner it can be transferred to other places, to serve the same temporary use, the better.

—JAMES HUDSON TAYLOR

See also Evangelism

OBEDIENCE ～

The best measure of spiritual life is not ecstasies but obedience.

—OSWALD CHAMBERS

What our Lord said about cross-bearing and obedience is not in the fine type. It is in bold print on the face of the contract.

—VANCE HAVNER

Learn to obey. Only he who obeys a rhythm superior to his own is free.

—NIKOS KAZANTZAKIS

An office-bearer who wants something other than to obey his King is unfit to bear his office.

—ABRAHAM KUYPER

Nothing is really lost by a life of sacrifice; everything is lost by failure to obey God's call.

—HENRY PARRY LIDDON

For obedience is not a stodgy plodding in the ruts of religion, it is a hopeful race toward God's promises.

—EUGENE PETERSON

God has given his order: that is an end of it. There is no need for argument.

—JAMES S. STEWART

Greatness in the kingdom of God is measured in terms of obedience.

—JOHN STOTT

When you suffer and lose, that does not mean you are being disobedient. In fact, it might mean you're right in the center of his will. The path of obedience is often marked by times of suffering and loss.

—CHARLES SWINDOLL

When we have the feeling that on some occasion we have disobeyed God, it simply means that for a time we have ceased to desire obedience.

—SIMONE WEIL

[For most people] the voice of their neighbors is louder than the voice of God.

—H. G. WELLS

PRAYER ~

The purpose of prayer is to leave us alone with God.

—LEO BAECK

The man who says his prayers in the evening is a captain posting his sentries. After that, he can sleep.

—CHARLES BAUDELAIRE

Pray: To ask that the laws of the universe be annulled in behalf of a single petitioner confessedly unworthy.

—AMBROSE BIERCE

When we pray it is far more important to pray with a sense of the greatness of God than with a sense of the greatness of the problem.

—EVANGELINE BLOOD

Prayer for many is like a foreign land. When we go there, we go as tourists. Like most tourists, we feel uncomfortable and out of place. Like most tourists, we therefore move on before too long and go somewhere else.
—ROBERT MCAFEE BROWN

The best prayers have often more groans than words.

—JOHN BUNYAN

The prayer, "Thy kingdom come," if we only knew it, is asking God to conduct a major operation.

—GEORGE BUTTRICK

Prayer—secret, fervent, believing prayer—lies at the root of all personal godliness.
—WILLIAM CAREY

The real business of your life as a saved soul is intercessory prayer.
—OSWALD CHAMBERS

We little know the things for which we pray.

—GEOFFREY CHAUCER

And Satan trembles when he sees
The weakest saint upon his knees.
—WILLIAM COWPER

Keep praying, but be thankful that God's answers are wiser than your prayers.
—WILLIAM CULBERTSON

He didn't actually accuse God of inefficiency, but when he prayed his tone was loud and angry, like that of a dissatisfied guest in a carelessly managed hotel.
—CLARENCE DAY

Whoever wrestles with God in prayer puts his whole life at stake.

—JACQUES ELLUL

Prayer is opening ourselves to God so that he can open us to others.

—LOUIS EVELY

To be straightforward with God is neither an easy nor a common grace.

—FREDERICK WILLIAM FABER

The worst sin is prayerlessness.

—P. T. FORSYTH

We are working with God to determine the future! Certain things will happen in history if we pray rightly. We are to change the world by prayer.

—RICHARD FOSTER

Pray, pray very much; but beware of telling God what you want.

—FRENCH PROVERB

The fewer the words, the better the prayer.

—GERMAN PROVERB

Pray as though no work would help, and work as though no prayer would help.

—GERMAN PROVERB

Prayer is the key of the morning and the bolt of the evening.

—MATTHEW HENRY

Silence is the language God speaks, and everything else is a bad translation.

—THOMAS KEATING

Prayer does not change God, but it changes him who prays.

—SØREN KIERKEGAARD

The trouble with nearly everybody who prays is that he says "Amen" and runs away before God has a chance to reply. Listening to God is far more important than giving him your ideas.

—FRANK LAUBACH

There is nothing that makes us love a man so much as praying for him.

—WILLIAM LAW

I have been driven many times to my knees by the overwhelming conviction that I had nowhere else to go. My own wisdom, and that of all about me, seemed insufficient for the day.

—ABRAHAM LINCOLN

I have so much business I cannot get on without spending three hours daily in prayer.

—MARTIN LUTHER

The value of persistent prayer is not that he will hear us . . . but that we will finally hear him.

—WILLIAM MCGILL

In the spiritual life there are no tricks and no short cuts. . . . One cannot begin to face the real difficulties of the life of prayer and meditation unless one is first perfectly content to be a beginner and really experience oneself as one who knows little or nothing, and has a desperate need to learn the bare rudiments.

—THOMAS MERTON

Prayer means yearning for the simple presence of God, for a personal understanding of his word, for knowledge of his will and for capacity to hear and obey him.

—THOMAS MERTON

I'd rather be able to pray than be a great preacher; Jesus Christ never taught his disciples how to preach but only how to pray.

—D. L. MOODY

Every evening I turn my troubles over to God—he's going to be up all night anyway.

—DONALD J. MORGAN

All prayers are answered. We need to distinguish between a prayer unanswered and one not answered how or when we would like it to be.

—LLOYD OGILVIE

Of all human activities, man's listening to God is the supreme act of his reasoning and will.

—POPE PAUL VI

[O]ne of the main reasons so many of God's children don't have a significant prayer life is not so much that we don't want to, but that we don't plan to. . . . We get up day after day and realize that significant times of prayer should be part of our life, but nothing's ever ready. We don't know where to go. Nothing has been planned. No time. No place. No procedure. . . . If you want renewal in your life of prayer you must *plan* to see it.

—JOHN PIPER

Man is great only when he is kneeling.

—POPE PIUS XII

I used to write in my daily calendar "7-7:30 a.m.—Prayer." But many times I passed that up. It was one more thing to pass by that day. Now I write "7-7:30—God." Somehow that's a little harder to neglect.

—DON POSTEMA

Pray to God but keep rowing to the shore.

—RUSSIAN PROVERB

My words fly up, my thoughts remain below:
Words without thoughts never to heaven go.

—WILLIAM SHAKESPEARE, *HAMLET*

Pray as if everything depended upon God and work as if everything depended on man.

—FRANCIS SPELLMAN (ALSO ATTRIBUTED TO OTHERS)

We cannot all argue, but we can all pray; we cannot all be leaders, but we can all be pleaders; we cannot all be mighty in rhetoric, but we can all be prevalent in prayer. I would sooner see you eloquent with God than with men.

—CHARLES HADDON SPURGEON

If Christ himself needed to retire from time to time to the mountain-top to pray, lesser men need not be ashamed to acknowledge that necessity.

—B. H. STREETER

Prayer is dangerous business. Results do come.

—G. CHRISTIE SWAIN

Whatsoever we beg of God, let us also work for it.

—JEREMY TAYLOR

More things are wrought by prayer than this world dreams of.

—ALFRED, LORD TENNYSON

We are too busy to pray, and so we are too busy to have power. We have a great deal of activity but we accomplish little; many services, but few conversions; much machinery but few results.

—R. A. TORREY

As a man prays, so is he.

—A. W. TOZER

We must not conceive of prayer as an overcoming of God's reluctance, but as a laying hold of his highest willingness.

—RICHARD CHENEVIX TRENCH

Deep down in me I knowed it was a lie, and he knowed it. You can't pray a lie—I found that out.

—MARK TWAIN

Too many people pray only for emergency rations rather than asking God for daily bread.

—UNKNOWN

What men usually ask of God when they pray is that two and two not make four.

—UNKNOWN

God does nothing but in answer to prayer.

—JOHN WESLEY

Whether you like it or no, read and pray daily. It is for your life; there is no other way; else you will be a trifler all your days.

—JOHN WESLEY

PRAYERS ~

Lord, deliver me from ego.

—ROGER AXTELL

Grant that this day we fall into no sin, neither run into any kind of danger.

—BOOK OF COMMON PRAYER

O Lord, be thou merciful
For I am going into the forest.

—EUROPEAN PRAYER

Teach us, good Lord, to serve Thee as Thou deservest: to give and not to count the cost; to fight and not to heed the wounds; to toil and not to seek for rest; to labor and not to ask for any reward save that of knowing we do Thy will.

—ST. IGNATIUS OF LOYOLA

Keep us safe from every ill,
Every mishap, every pain,
Let no animals attack us.
Lord, bring us safely home.

—KALAHARI BUSHMAN PRAYER

From the cowardice that dare not face new truths,
From the laziness that is contented with half truth,
From the arrogance that thinks it knows all truth,
Good Lord, deliver me.

—KENYAN PRAYER

Lord, send me anywhere, only go with me. Lay any burden on me, only sustain me. Sever any ties but the tie that binds me to thy service and to thy heart.

—DAVID LIVINGSTONE

O Lord, forgive me for what I have been, sanctify what I am, and order what I shall be.

—FREDERICK MACNUTT

These things, good Lord, that we pray for, give us thy grace to labor for.

—THOMAS MOORE

Now I lay me down to sleep,
I pray the Lord my soul to keep;
If I should die before I wake,
I pray thee, Lord, my soul to take.

—*NEW ENGLAND PRIMER*, 1814

God grant me the serenity to accept the things I cannot change, courage to change the things I can, and wisdom to know the difference.

—FRIEDRICH CHRISTOPH OETINGER
(ALSO ATTRIBUTED TO OTHERS)

Dear God: make the bad people good and all the good people nice.

—PRAYER OF A SMALL GIRL

God bless mother and daddy, my brother and sister, and save the king. And, oh God, take care of yourself, because if anything happens to you, we're all sunk.

—ADLAI E. STEVENSON

Guide me, O Lord, in all the changes and varieties of the world; that in all things that shall happen, I may have an evenness and tranquility of spirit; that my soul may be wholly resigned to Thy divinest will and pleasure, never murmuring at Thy gentle chastisements and fatherly correction.

—JEREMY TAYLOR

Dear God: Please help me be the person my dog thinks I am.

—UNKNOWN

Lord, may I live each day as though Christ died yesterday, rose again today, and is coming again tomorrow.

—UNKNOWN

Lord, today let me see how you work through the life and character of someone I don't really like and help me to love them for it.

—UNKNOWN

So far today, God, I've done all right. I haven't gossiped; lost my temper; been greedy, grumpy, nasty, selfish or even overindulgent. I'm really glad about that. But, in a few minutes, God, I'm going to get out of bed and from then on I'm probably going to need a lot more help. Thank you.

—UNKNOWN

PREACHING & SERMONS

The Christian church does not need more popular preaching, but more unpopular preaching.

—WALTER RUSSELL BOWIE

To love to preach is one thing—to love those to whom we preach, quite another.

—RICHARD CECIL

He preaches well that lives well.

—MIGUEL DE CERVANTES

Sermons remain one of the last forms of public discourse where it is culturally forbidden to talk back.

—HARVEY COX

The test of a preacher is that his congregation goes away saying, not "What a lovely sermon!" but "I will do something."

—ST. FRANCIS DE SALES

If it is possible to train elephants to dance, lions to play, and leopards to hunt, it should be possible to teach preachers to preach.

—ERASMUS

Preaching is effective as long as the preacher expects something to happen—not because of the sermon, not even because of the preacher, but because of God.

—JOHN E. HINES

. . . the Rev. Mr. Wiggin's sermons were about as entertaining and convincing as a pilot's voice in the intercom, explaining technical difficulties while the plane plummets toward the earth and the stewardesses are screaming. . . .

—JOHN IRVING,
A PRAYER FOR OWEN MEANY

When a minister stands in front of people, he is interrupting what the people have come to church for. He had better have a good reason for doing that. Otherwise, he shouldn't stand up and talk. We don't need the minister unless he has something that the Spirit has put in his heart to say.

—GARRISON KEILLOR

Only the sinner has the right to preach.

—CHRISTOPHER MORLEY

Good sermons happen when flint strikes steel—when the flint of a person's experience strikes the steel of the Word of God.

—HADDON ROBINSON

Preachers say, Do as I say, not as I do. But if the physician had the same disease upon him that I have, and he should bid me do one thing and himself do quite another, could I believe him?

—JOHN SELDEN

Most preachers handle sin as they would handle snakes, at arm's length and with no greater intimacy and for no longer time than is absolutely necessary.

—SAM SHOEMAKER

Few sinners are saved after the first twenty minutes of a sermon.

—MARK TWAIN

Don't judge the quality of the gasoline by the filling station attendant.

—UNKNOWN

Great preaching depends on great listening.

—ALAN WALKER

Preach not because you have to say something but because you have something to say.

—RICHARD WHATELY

RELATIONSHIPS ～

Anyone without a soul friend is like a body without a head.

—CELTIC SAYING

There is no such thing as an insignificant human being. To treat people that way is a kind of sin and there's no reason for it. None.

—DEBBI FIELDS

Friends are God's apologies for relations.

—HUGH KINGSMILL

There are no ordinary people. You have never talked to an ordinary mortal. . . . It is immortals whom we joke with, work with, marry, snub and exploit—immortal horrors or everlasting splendors. . . . Next to the Blessed Sacrament itself, your neighbor is the holiest object presented to your senses.

—C. S. LEWIS

A man must not choose his neighbor; he must take the neighbor that God sends him. The neighbor is just the man who is next to you at the moment, the man with whom any business has brought you into contact.

—GEORGE MACDONALD

Loneliness is the first thing which God's eye named not good.

—JOHN MILTON

Community is the place where God completes our lives with his joy.

—HENRI NOUWEN

James B. Pratt, in *India and its Faiths*, tells the story of the Indian who, at the time of the mutiny, greeted the soldier about to bayonet him with the extraordinary words, "And thou too art divine."

—ALAN PATON

A true friend is the gift of God, and he only who made hearts can unite them.

—ROBERT SOUTH

If this is God's world there are no unimportant people.

—GEORGE THOMAS

Never believe anything bad about anybody unless you positively know it to be true; never tell even that unless you feel it is absolutely necessary—and that God is listening while you tell it.

—HENRY VAN DYKE

See also Home, Family, and Marriage

RELIGION &
RELIGIOUS FREEDOM ～

A religion that is small enough for our understanding is not great enough for our need.

—A. J. BALFOUR

A culture obsessed with technology will come to value personal convenience above almost all else, and ours does. . . . Religion tends to be strongest when life is hard . . . a person whose main difficulty is not crop failure but video breakdown has less need of the consolations and promises of religion.

—ROBERT BORK

Never trust anybody not of sound religion, for he that is false to God can never be true to man.

—LORD BURLEIGH

Let your religion be less of a theory and more of a love affair.

—G. K. CHESTERTON

You have to be very religious to change your religion.

—COMTESSE DIANE

Religion is more like a response to a friend than it is like obedience to an expert.

—AUSTIN FARRER

Religion is the best armor in the world but the worst cloak.

—THOMAS FULLER

True religion is betting one's life that there is a God.

—DONALD HANKEY

I would give nothing for that man's religion, whose very dog, and cat are not the better for it.

—ROWLAND HILL

Religion is a way of walking, not a way of talking.

—WILLIAM R. INGE

Religions are man's search for God; the gospel is God's search for man. There are many religions, but one gospel.

—E. STANLEY JONES

Religion . . . is the opium of the people.

—KARL MARX
(BUT PREVIOUSLY ATTRIBUTED TO HEINRICH HEINE)

We have just enough religion to make us hate, but not enough to make us love one another.

—JONATHAN SWIFT

It is certainly no part of religion to compel religion.

—TERTULLIAN

To some people religious freedom means the choice of churches which they may stay away from.

—UNKNOWN

Religion must provide the believer an answer when he asks why there are rich and poor, violence and justice, war and peace, or it will force him to look for an answer elsewhere.

—LUDWIG VON MISES

REPENTANCE ~

True repentance is to cease from sin.

—St. Ambrose

"Oh God, if I were sure I were to die tonight I would repent at once." It is the commonest prayer in all languages.

—J. M. Barrie

If ever you cease to know the virtue of repentance, you are in darkness.

—Oswald Chambers

Sleep with clean hands, either kept clean all day by integrity or washed clean at night by repentance.

—John Donne

You cannot repent too soon, because you do not know how soon it may be too late.

—Thomas Fuller

Confession is the first step to repentance.

—Edmund Gayton

Repentance is always difficult, and the difficulty grows still greater by delay.

—Samuel Johnson

Repentance was perhaps best defined by a small girl: "It's to be sorry enough to quit."

—C. H. Kilmer

Remorse is impotent; it will sin again. Only repentance is strong; it can end everything.

—Henry Miller

Repentance is not an emotion. It is not feeling sorry for your sins. It is a decision. It is deciding that you have been wrong in supposing that you could manage your own life and be your own god. . . . Repentance is a decision to follow Jesus Christ and become his pilgrim in the path of peace.

—EUGENE PETERSON

There is no good news in the gospel unless we first admit the bad news about ourselves.

—JAMES REAPSOME

God keeps the wicked to give them time to repent.

—SOPHIE SÉGUR

There is in repentance this great mystery—that we may fly fastest home on broken wing.

—WILLIAM L. SULLIVAN

True repentance hates the sin, and not merely the penalty; and it hates the sin most of all because it has discovered and felt God's love.

—W. M. TAYLOR

There is no repentance in the grave.

—ISAAC WATTS

Repentance, contrary to popular misconception, is not a heroic first step I make toward Christ nor is it a feeling-sorry-for my sins. It is the divine gift of being able to be turned toward truth.

—WILLIAM WILLIMON

A Christian is a man who feels
Repentance on Sunday
For what he did on Saturday
And is going to do on Monday.

—THOMAS RUSSELL YBARRA

To repent is not to feel bad but to think differently.

—JOHN YODER

RESISTING THE WORLD ∾

The self is the modern substitute for the soul.

—ALLAN BLOOM

I fear that Christians who stand with only one leg upon earth
also stand with only one leg in heaven.

—DIETRICH BONHOEFFER

The socially prescribed affluent, middle-class lifestyle has
become so normative in our churches that we discern little
conflict between it and the Christian lifestyle prescribed in the
New Testament.

—TONY CAMPOLO

It is not the ship in the water but the water in the ship that
sinks it. So it is not the Christian in the world but the world
in the Christian that constitutes the danger.

—J. WILBUR CHAPMAN

Paganism holds all the most valuable advertising space.

—T. S. ELIOT

In the beginning the church was a fellowship of men and women centering on the living Christ. Then the church moved to Greece, where it became a philosophy. Then it moved to Rome, where it became an institution. Next it moved to Europe, where it became a culture, and, finally, it moved to America, where it became an enterprise.

—RICHARD HALVERSON

The church which is married to the spirit of its age will find itself a widow in the next.

—WILLIAM R. INGE

God has been replaced, as he has all over the West, with respectability and air conditioning.

—LEROI JONES

The church once changed society. It was then a thermostat of society. But today . . . the church is merely a thermometer, which measures rather than molds popular opinion.

—MARTIN LUTHER KING, JR.

Too often an institution serves to bless the majority opinion. Today when too many move to the rhythmic beat of the status quo, whoever would be a Christian must be a nonconformist.

—MARTIN LUTHER KING, JR.

They sought the world, and it fled them not.

—JOHN KNOX, ON CERTAIN PASTORS OF HIS DAY

Worldliness is not, in the last analysis, love of possessions, or the habit of courting great personages. It is simply the weakness of fiber which makes us take our standards from the society around us.

—RONALD KNOX

The most recent goal of positive thinking, personal fulfill-
ment, seems to correspond with certain aspects of biblical
faith. Jesus promised an abundant life. What more could we
ask? So we threw open the doors of the sanctuary to the
human potential movement (the quest for a maximized *me*)
and warmly extended to it the right hand of fellowship.

—D. W. McCullough

It is curious to realize that people like you and me, who set
such store by being settled and secure, should worship a God
whose revelation was to nomads and wanderers. We try to
domesticate God, try to get God to settle down with us—but
never succeed.

—Barbara Moorman

The only ultimate disaster that can befall us is to feel ourselves
at home on this earth.

—Malcolm Muggeridge

Being a Christian in America doesn't require a great cost. You
can be a Christian and fully participate in the secular culture.
I have a sense that, more and more, being a Christian in this
country will require a choice. The Christian will have to be
willing to make big sacrifices. . . . Right now, in this culture,
you can have your cake and eat it too. But that is an illusion.
You cannot be a fat sprinter. If you want to sprint to the
Kingdom, you had better be lean.

—Henri Nouwen

The culture most lost to the gospel is our own. . . . It's a culture that can't say two sentences without referencing a TV show or a pop song, and that can't remember what it was like to have to *get up* and change channels. It's a culture more likely to have a body part pierced than it is to know why Sarah laughed. . . . It's a culture that we stopped evangelizing, and have instead declared a culture war upon.

—DWIGHT OZARD

O Lord, grant that we may not be conformed to the world, but may love it and serve it. Grant we may never shrink from being the instruments of thy peace because of the judgment of the world. Grant that we may love thee without fear of the world, grant that we may never believe that the inexpressible majesty of thyself may be found in any power of this earth.

—ALAN PATON

It is interesting to listen to the comments that outsiders, particularly those from Third World countries, make on the religion they observe in North America. What they notice mostly is the greed, the silliness, the narcissism. They appreciate the size and prosperity of our churches, the energy and the technology, but they wonder at the conspicuous absence of the cross, the phobic avoidance of suffering, the puzzling indifference to community and relationships of intimacy.

—EUGENE PETERSON

It is time that the Christian reacquire the consciousness of belonging to a minority and of often being in opposition to what is obvious, plausible and natural for that mentality which the New Testament calls . . . the "spirit of the world." It is time to find again the courage of nonconformism, the capacity to oppose many of the trends of the surrounding culture.

—JOSEPH RATZINGER

Tell me what the world is saying now and I'll tell you what the church will be saying seven years from now.

—FRANCIS SCHAEFFER

One of the commonest compromises that have been made is for the world to allow the church to be at peace in proclaiming what may be called its philosophical paradoxes provided that it keeps quiet about its moral ones.

—WILLIAM TEMPLE

Perhaps one of our problems as Christians is that we don't see ourselves as fish out of water. We've got too used to swimming along with the rest of the world.

—UNKNOWN

Secularism is the practice of the absence of God.

—UNKNOWN

Worldliness is what any particular culture does to make sin look normal and righteousness look strange.

—DAVID WELLS

See also Materialism, Money, and Possessions;
Success and Failure

SABBATH ～

Sunday clears away the rust of the whole week.

—JOSEPH ADDISON

There are many people who think that Sunday is a sponge to wipe out all the sins of the week.

—HENRY WARD BEECHER

The sabbath is an oasis in time.

—ABRAHAM JOSHUA HESCHEL

Day of the Lord, as all our days should be!

—HENRY WADSWORTH LONGFELLOW

Take the Sunday with you through the week, and sweeten with it all the other days.

—HENRY WADSWORTH LONGFELLOW

Do not let Sunday be taken from you. . . . If your soul has no Sunday, it becomes an orphan.

—ALBERT SCHWEITZER

The Lord's day is the shadow of Christ on the hot highway of time.

—ROBERT E. SPEER

There is probably no more accurate test of one's Christian devotion than one's attitude toward, and conduct on, the Lord's day.

—RICHARD TAYLOR

The longer I live the more highly do I estimate the Christian sabbath, and the more grateful do I feel to those who impress its importance on the community.

—DANIEL WEBSTER

What a child is taught on Sunday it will remember on Monday.

—WELSH PROVERB

SALVATION

He who created us without our help will not save us without our consent.

—ST. AUGUSTINE

There is no salvation outside the church.

—ST. AUGUSTINE

Salvation is not putting a man into heaven but putting heaven into a man.

—MALTBIE D. BABCOCK

God never draws anyone to himself by force and violence. He wishes all men to be saved, but forces no one.

—JOHN CHRYSOSTOM

No man was ever scared into heaven.

—THOMAS FULLER

Diverse are the ways by which men come to Christ. And great is the temptation to judge others if they do not have mud put on their eyes and go to Siloam exactly as we did.

—VANCE HAVNER

Salvation is not so much a matter of doing as of appreciating what God has done.

—RICHARD F. LOVELACE

Being saved is not the end of our journey but it is the end of our wandering.

—WILLIAM S. STODDARD

I can contribute nothing to my own salvation, except the sin from which I need to be redeemed.

—WILLIAM TEMPLE

I felt my heart strangely warmed. I felt I did trust in Christ, Christ alone for my salvation; and an assurance was given me that he had taken away my sins, even mine, and saved me from the law of sin and death.

—JOHN WESLEY

Salvation is so simple that we overlook it; so profound that we never comprehend it; so free we can't believe it.

—PAUL WHITE

SATAN ～

Old Satan couldn't get along without plenty of help.

—AFRICAN AMERICAN PROVERB

Renounce the devil and all his works.

—BOOK OF COMMON PRAYER

We must remember that Satan has his miracles too.

—JOHN CALVIN

He who sups with the devil should have a long spoon.

—ENGLISH PROVERB

All the demons we shall meet are doomed and damned by the Christ who ruined them.

—P. T. FORSYTH

When we do ill, the Devil tempts us; when we do nothing, we tempt him.

—THOMAS FULLER

One is always wrong to open a conversation with the Devil, for, however he goes about it, he always insists on having the last word.

—ANDRÉ GIDE

If I take on Jesus as my Lord, I take on the devil as my enemy.

—MICHAEL GREEN

If the devil could be persuaded to write a bible, he would title it "You Only Live Once."

—SYDNEY HARRIS

It is so stupid of modern civilization to have given up believing in the devil when he is the only explanation of it.

—RONALD KNOX

The devil is easy to identify. He appears when you're terribly tired and makes a very reasonable request which you know you shouldn't grant.

—FIORELLO LA GUARDIA

There are two equal and opposite errors into which our race can fall about the devils. One is to disbelieve in their existence. The other is to believe, and to feel an excessive and unhealthy interest in them. They themselves are equally pleased by both errors, and hail a materialist or a magician with the same delight.

—C. S. LEWIS

Evil is near. Sometimes late at night the air grows strongly clammy and cold around me. I feel it brushing me. All that the devil asks is acquiescence . . . not struggle, not conflict. Acquiescence.

—SUZANNE MASSIE

Satan is especially active at the times of danger.

—RASHI

The devil hath power to assume a pleasing shape.

—WILLIAM SHAKESPEARE, *HAMLET*

The devil is a better theologian than any of us and is a devil still.

—A. W. TOZER

Satan is never too busy to rock the cradle of a sleeping Christian.

—UNKNOWN

Satan envies man's happiness. To see a clod of dust so near to God, and himself, once a glorious angel, cast out of heavenly paradise, makes him pursue mankind with inveterate hatred.

—THOMAS WATSON

For Satan finds some mischief still for idle hands to do.

—ISAAC WATTS

I am more and more convinced that the devil himself desires nothing more than that the people should be half-awakened and then left to fall asleep again.

—JOHN WESLEY

The devil never tempts us with more success than when he tempts us with a sight of our own good actions.

—THOMAS WILSON

Look at the parking lot outside any church. If you see Lexuses and Cadillacs, you won't hear Satan preached inside. If you see a lot of pickup trucks, you will.

—ROBERT WUTHNOW

See also Temptation

SERVICE ~

Learn the lesson that, if you are to do the work of a prophet, what you need is not a scepter but a hoe.

—BERNARD OF CLAIRVAUX

It is part of the discipline of humility that we must not spare our hand where it can perform a service and that we do not assume that our schedule is our own to manage, but allow it to be arranged by God.

—DIETRICH BONHOEFFER

Attempt great things for God. Expect great things from God.

—WILLIAM CAREY

I reckon on you for extreme service, with no complaining on your part and no explanation on mine.

—OSWALD CHAMBERS, ON GOD WORKING THROUGH US

Never allow the thought, "I am of no use where I am." You certainly can be of no use where you are not.

—OSWALD CHAMBERS

There is nothing small in the service of God.

—ST. FRANCIS DE SALES

This may be the day God gives me a great opportunity to serve someone who needs help from me.

—BILL GROSZ

Ministry is what we leave in our wake as we follow Jesus.

—GERALD HARTIS

You can tell whether you are becoming a servant by how you act when people treat you like one.

—GORDON MACDONALD
(ALSO ATTRIBUTED TO OTHERS)

In the kingdom of God service is not a stepping-stone to nobility: it *is* nobility, the only kind of nobility that is recognized.

—T. W. MANSON

They also serve who only stand and wait.

—JOHN MILTON

There are many of us that are willing to do great things for the Lord, but few of us are willing to do the little things.

—D. L. MOODY

Serve God and be cheerful.

—MOTTO OF LICHFIELD CATHEDRAL, ENGLAND

O Lord, help us to be masters of ourselves, that we may be servants of others.

—ALEXANDER PATERSON

Many folks want to serve God, but only as advisers.

—MONIQUE RYSAVY

Nothing seems tiresome or painful when you are working for a Master who pays well; who rewards even a cup of cold water given for love of him.

—ST. DOMINIC SAVIO

I am a little pencil in the hand of a writing God who is sending a love letter to the world.

—MOTHER TERESA

There is not one single passage in the Old Testament or the New Testament where the filling with the Holy Spirit is spoken of and not connected with the testimony of service.

—R. A. TORREY

If you wish to be a leader you will be frustrated, for very few people wish to be led. If you aim to be a servant, you will never be frustrated.

—FRANK F. WARREN

SEX & SEXUALITY ∽

I have often wondered why theology and biology seem to contradict each other. God says NO at exactly the time our bodies say GO. Did God get confused in the creation process? I believe God intends that we learn control and discipline. We have to learn this in other ways, such as coordinating and disciplining growing muscles when we're children. Why not hormones? Maybe God knows what he's doing after all!

—KEITH ANDERSON

Give me chastity and continence, but not yet!

—ST. AUGUSTINE

The essence of chastity is not the suppression of lust, but the total orientation of one's life toward a goal.

—DIETRICH BONHOEFFER

Modern man speaks of intercourse as "having sex." However, the Scriptures never speak this way. In Biblical language, a man "knows" his wife. It is not an act; it is a relationship.

—Paul Bubna

Whenever Christ was confronted by people in sexual disarray, he took good care to safeguard sexuality by reminding them that they had to avoid sin; that is to say to use their sexuality in a fully human way.

—Jack Dominian

There's no question about it. The sex-related issues are going to be the most important issues facing all churches in the foreseeable future. Abortion, AIDS, premarital sex, homosexuality, all those are going to be at the vortex.

—George H. Gallup, Jr.

There is no getting away from it: the old Christian rule is "Either marriage, with complete faithfulness to your partner, or else total abstinence." Chastity is the most unpopular of our Christian virtues.

—C. S. Lewis

Christian teaching about sex is by no means clear in detail, but what shines through with pellucid clarity throughout the Christian tradition is that sex is a very holy subject.

—Geddes MacGregor

To be a celibate means to be empty for God, to be free and open for his presence, to be available for his service.

—Henri Nouwen

The greatest illusion of lovers is to believe that the intensity of their sexual attraction is the guarantee of the perpetuity of their love. It is because of this failure to distinguish between the glandular and the spiritual . . . that marriages are so full of deception.

—FULTON SHEEN

I have a hunch that the last institution around at this moment which has a high doctrine of sex is the church.

—WILLIAM SWING

Sex is no test of love, for it is precisely the very thing that one wants to test that is destroyed by the testing.

—WALTER TROBISCH

How strangely on modern ears falls the notion that lust—sexual desire that wells up in us as involuntarily as saliva—in itself is wicked.

—JOHN UPDIKE

See also Home, Family, and Marriage; Love

SIN & SINNERS ～

Sin is the best news there is, the best news there could be in our predicament. Because with sin, there's a way out. There's the possibility of repentance. You can't repent of confusion or psychological flaws inflicted by your parents—you're stuck with them. But you can repent of sin. Sin and repentance are the only grounds for hope and joy. . . . You can be born again.

—JOHN ALEXANDER

Sin we have explained away;
Unluckily, the sinners stay.

—William Allingham

All sin tends to be addictive, and the terminal point of addiction is what is called damnation.

—W. H. Auden

No one sins by an act he cannot avoid.

—St. Augustine

Men have never been good, they are not good, they never will be good.

—Karl Barth

Sin: Something that used to be called a sin; now it's called a complex.

—Eva Bartok

Our sense of sin is in proportion to our nearness to God.

—Thomas D. Bernard

No deed is complete in itself. No evil act can be confined to the hour of its doing. Sin is eminently productive. Each act of wickedness forms a link in a chain, which, unless God breaks it in grace, tangles with eternity.

—E. M. Blaiklock

It is astonishing how soon the whole conscience begins to unravel, if a single stitch drops; one little sin indulged makes a hole you could put your head through.

—Charles Buxton

Pride, covetousness, lust, anger, gluttony, envy and sloth are the seven capital sins.

—A Catechism of Christian Doctrine
for General Use

Each sin has its own excuse.

—CZECH PROVERB

The Anglo-Saxon conscience does not prevent the Anglo-Saxon from sinning, it merely prevents him from enjoying his sin.

—SALVADOR DE MADARIAGA

There was a time when we were afraid of being caught doing something sinful in front of our ministers. Now we are afraid of being immature in front of our therapists.

—PETER DE VRIES

There are no incorrigible sinners; God has no permanent problem children.

—NELS F. S. FERRE

We are not stray sheep or wandering prodigals even, but rebels taken with weapons in our hands.

—P. T. FORSYTH

Sin causes the cup of joy to spring a leak.

—ROBERT E. HARRIS

Sin is the canoe that will land you in hell.

—HAWAIIAN PROVERB

Fashions in sin change.

—LILLIAN HELLMAN

A sin, even if committed by many, remains a sin.

—HUNGARIAN PROVERB

Adam ate the apple and our teeth still ache.

—HUNGARIAN PROVERB

[Sin:] The breaking of one's integrity.

—D. H. LAWRENCE

The human heart, even the redeemed heart, has an allergy to God.

—RICHARD F. LOVELACE

All sin, whatever the degree, is equal in its capacity to separate us from God's heart of love.

—GEORGE MACDONALD

We are too Christian really to enjoy sinning, and too fond of sinning really to enjoy Christianity. Most of us know perfectly well what we ought to do; our trouble is that we do not want to do it.

—PETER MARSHALL

Sin . . . has been made not only ugly but passé. People are no longer sinful, they are only immature or underprivileged or, more particularly, sick.

—PHYLLIS MCGINLEY, 1959

Original sin is the only empirically verifiable Christian doctrine.

—RICHARD NEUHAUS

All human sin seems so much worse in its consequences than in its intentions.

—REINHOLD NIEBUHR

Original sin is that thing about man which makes him capable of conceiving of his own perfection and incapable of achieving it.

—REINHOLD NIEBUHR

There are only two kinds of men: the righteous who believe themselves sinners, and the rest, sinners, who believe themselves righteous.

—BLAISE PASCAL

Hurt not your conscience with any known sin.

—SAMUEL RUTHERFORD

It makes a great difference whether a person is unwilling to sin, or does not know how.

—SENECA

The sins that we should hate most are not those of our neighbor but our own. These are the only sins over which God has given us immediate power.

—RAPHAEL SIMON

Sin is disappointing. Whoever got out of sin half as much pleasure as he expected?

—IGNATIUS SMITH

It is no disgrace that the soiling of the day's life affects our souls; it is disgrace if we suffer it to remain uncleansed and accept the defilement. So we ask God the cleansing from "the dust of the way."

—GEORGE STEWART

We don't call it sin today—we call it self-expression.

—BARONESS STOCKS

Sin cannot be undone, only forgiven.

—IGOR STRAVINSKY

It is fitting for a great God to forgive great sinners.

—THE TALMUD

Rabbi Akiba said: "In the beginning, sin is like a thread of a spider's web; but in the end, it becomes like the cable of a ship."

—THE TALMUD

No sin is small. No grain of sand is small in the mechanism of a watch.

—JEREMY TAYLOR

The blood of Jesus never cleansed an excuse.

—CORRIE TEN BOOM

Don't let your sin turn into bad habits.

—TERESA OF AVILA

It is true that we cannot be free from sin, but at least let our sins not always be the same.

—TERESA OF AVILA

Sin and evil must be seen as enemies to be fought rather than problems to be solved.

—UNKNOWN

To sin is to poison the public reservoir.

—LESLIE D. WEATHERHEAD

SOCIAL ISSUES ∾

Stewardship is more than setting up soup kitchens and overnight shelters. It is good and right that we reach into the river of despair and rescue people who are drowning. But it is time to move upstream and see who's throwing them in.

—EDMOND BROWNING

You can't divorce religious belief and public service. . . . I've never detected any conflict between God's will and my political duty. If you violate one you violate the other.

—JIMMY CARTER

Even if a man were in rapture like St. Paul and knew of a man who was in need of food, he would do better by feeding him than by remaining in ecstasy.

—MEISTER ECKHART

There is one test, and one only, of the extent of our love for him, and it is a very uncomfortable one. How have we handled the poor?

—MICHAEL GREEN

The white Christian church never raised to the heights of Christ. It stayed within the limits of culture.

—JESSE JACKSON

I tremble for my country when I reflect that God is just.

—THOMAS JEFFERSON

The church must be reminded that it is not the master or the servant of the state, but rather its conscience.

—MARTIN LUTHER KING, JR.

If you preach the gospel in all aspects with the exception of the issues which deal specifically with your time you are not preaching the gospel at all.

—MARTIN LUTHER

The tendency to claim God as an ally for our partisan values and ends is . . . the source of all religious fanaticism.

—REINHOLD NIEBUHR

You are a Christian only so long as you constantly pose critical questions to the society you live in . . . so long as you stay unsatisfied with the status quo and keep saying that a new world is yet to come.

—HENRI NOUWEN

The 11 o'clock hour on Sunday is the most segregated hour in American life.

—JAMES A. PIKE

History shows that, in our culture at least, when religious leaders enter into electoral politics, it is more likely that religion will be debased than that politics will be elevated.

—ANTHONY M. PILLA

The place of the church is not to change society but to change men and women who will then do the changing of society.

—DANIEL A. POLING

[I]f the Christ of scripture is our Lord, then we will refuse to be squeezed into the mold of our affluent, sinful culture. In an Age of Hunger Christians of necessity must be radical nonconformists. But nonconformity is painful. Only if we are thoroughly grounded in the scriptural view of possessions, wealth and poverty will we be capable of living an obedient lifestyle.

—RON SIDER

Prayer or no prayer, you can't eat out of an empty bowl.

—SLOVAKIAN PROVERB

Every Christian should be both conservative and radical; conservative in preserving the faith and radical in applying it.

—JOHN STOTT

Christianity is weakest when it is brought face to face with the color bar.

—HOWARD THOMAS

A church that is in solidarity with the poor can never become a wealthy church.

—DESMOND TUTU

A church which has nothing to say on political, economic and international issues abandons God and betrays the people.

—ALAN WALKER

See also The Church; Resisting the World

STEWARDSHIP & GIVING ~

Man should not consider his outward possessions as his own, but as common to all, so as to share them without hesitation when others are in need.

—THOMAS AQUINAS

Charity is no substitute for justice withheld.

—ST. AUGUSTINE

In charity there is no excess.

—FRANCIS BACON

Never respect men merely for their riches, but rather for their philanthropy; we do not value the sun for its height but for its use.

—GAMALIEL BAILEY

All our doings without charity are nothing worth.

—*BOOK OF COMMON PRAYER*

Tithe if you love Jesus. Any idiot can honk.

—BUMPER STICKER

I have never felt any hesitation in speaking to my congregation about money. . . . I thrill to it. I revel in it. I love to see the liberal enjoy it. I love to watch the stingy suffer.

—CLOVIS G. CHAPPELL

It is better to do a kindness near home than to go far to burn incense.

—CHINESE PROVERB

It was not an accident that seventeen of the thirty-six parables of our Lord had to do with property and stewardship.

—WILLIAM JAMES DAWSON

The love of God compels us to give.

—DOROTHY DAY

Isn't it better to have men being ungrateful than to miss the chance to do good?

—DENIS DIDEROT

Remember that when you leave this earth, you can take with you nothing that you have received—only what you have given: a full heart enriched by honest service, love, sacrifice and courage.

—ST. FRANCIS OF ASSISI

God has given us two hands—one to receive with and the other to give with. We are not cisterns made for hoarding; we are channels made for sharing.

—BILLY GRAHAM

Be not afraid to spend for charity and holy purposes; have confidence that God will return your gifts manifold.

—HASIDIC SAYING

It will not bother me in the hour of death to reflect that I have been "had for a sucker" by any number of imposters; but it would be a torment to know that one had refused even one person in need.

—C. S. LEWIS

The proper aim of giving is to put the recipient in a state where he no longer needs our gift.

—C. S. Lewis

The world asks, "How much does he give?" Christ asks, "Why does he give?"

—John Raleigh Mott

Proportion thy charity to the strength of thine estate, lest God proportion thine estate to the weakness of thy charity.

—Francis Quarles

Lots of people think they are being charitable if they give away their old clothes and things they don't want.

—Myrtle Reed

Stewardship is not leaving a tip on God's tablecloth; it is the confession of an unpayable debt at God's Calvary.

—Paul S. Rees

A . . . key axiom in giving is a simple one, namely, "You can't take it with you." Hence, you had better use it intelligently while you are on this earth. . . . One associate recently phrased it somewhat differently, saying, "You'll never see a hearse with a luggage rack."

—David Rockefeller

To think that payment of our tithe discharges our financial obligation to God is a gross deception. Man's responsibility in regard to money involves far more than ten per cent. It encompasses the whole of his money. It is as though we have been given an expense account by the Lord. We must be able to justify the items we charge against it.

—J. Oswald Sanders

Never measure your generosity by what you give, but rather by what you have left.

—FULTON SHEEN

Who gives to the poor, lends to God.

—SPANISH PROVERB

He who gives when he is asked has waited too long.

—*SUNSHINE* MAGAZINE

Charity often consists of a generous impulse to give away something for which we have no further use.

—UNKNOWN

Give to God and stop tipping him.

—UNKNOWN

It may have been better in the old days when charity was a virtue and not an industry.

—UNKNOWN

The word "alms" has no singular, as if to teach us that a solitary act of charity scarcely deserves the name.

—UNKNOWN

The dead carry with them to the grave in their clutched hands only that which they have given away.

—DEWITT WALLACE

When the possessor of heaven and earth brought you into being and placed you in this world, he placed you here not as an owner but as a steward—as such he entrusted you for a season with goods of various kinds—but the sole property of these still rests in him, nor can ever be alienated from him. As you are not your own but his, such is likewise all you enjoy.

—JOHN WESLEY

SUCCESS & FAILURE ∾

God has not asked us to be successful. He has asked us to be faithful.

—DAVID AUGSBURGER
(ALSO ATTRIBUTED TO OTHERS)

I know that any success apart from your Spirit is mere euphemism for failure.

—JOSEPH BAYLY

Our Lord said, "Feed my sheep." He did not say, "Count them."

—MARTIN BUBER

Try not to become a person of success but rather a person of value.

—ALBERT EINSTEIN

[Somehow] we never see God in failure, but only in success—a strange attitude for people who have the cross as the center of their faith.

—CHERYL FORBES

There is no success for the Christian other than being faithful to God's will and call.

—MARK HATFIELD

Success is living in such a way that you are using what God has given you—your intellect, abilities, and energy—to reach the purpose he intends for your life.

—KATHI HUDSON

Failure is the greatest opportunity to know who I really am.

—JOHN KILLINGER

God is a specialist: he is well able to work our failures into his plans. . . . Often the doorway to success is entered through the hallway of failure.

—ERWIN W. LUTZER

Success is not measured in possessions or by the state of our health. Success means to be where I am supposed to be—the right place at the right time and for the right reason—because of the purpose for my life that has its origins in God's love and faithfulness.

—EARL PALMER

Success can go to my head, and will unless I remember that it is God who accomplishes the work, and that he will be able to make out with other means whenever he cuts me down to size.

—CHARLES HADDON SPURGEON

There is no failure so great that a Christian cannot rise from it, there is no defeat so final that he cannot convert it into a victory.

—HELEN C. WHITE

SUFFERING & HARDSHIPS ⟿

I believe in the sun even when it is not shining. I believe in love even when not feeling it. I believe in God even when he is silent.

—ANONYMOUS INSCRIPTION ON THE WALL
OF A CELLAR IN COLOGNE, GERMANY,
WHERE JEWS HID FROM THE NAZIS

Thank the good God for having visited you through suffering; if we knew the value of suffering, we would ask for it.

—BROTHER ANDRÉ

Never judge God by suffering, but judge suffering by the cross.

—FATHER ANDREW

Sunshine without rain is the recipe for a desert.

—ARAB PROVERB

Then there was the woman who prayed for patience and God sent her a poor cook.

—HENRY WARD BEECHER

No wounds? No scar?
Can he have followed far
Who hath nor wounds, nor scar?

—AMY CARMICHAEL

There's nothing written in the Bible . . . that says if you believe in me, you ain't going to have no troubles.

—RAY CHARLES

God measures out affliction to our need.

—JOHN CHRYSOSTOM

He brought light out of darkness, not out of a lesser light; he can bring your summer out of winter, though you have no spring. . . . God comes to you, not as in the dawning of the day, not as in the bud of the spring, but as the sun at noon.

—JOHN DONNE

In America, Christians pray for the burden of suffering to be lifted from their backs. In the rest of the world, Christians pray for stronger backs so they can bear their suffering. It's why we look away from the bag lady on the street and to the displays in the store windows. Why we prefer going to the movies instead of to hospitals and nursing homes.

—DAVE DRAVECKY

In the mighty power of God, go on!

—GEORGE FOX

Just how much discord is required for God's formula for a successful life, no one knows, but it must have a use for it is always there.

—ELBERT HUBBARD

Have courage for the great sorrows of life, and patience for the small ones. And when you have laboriously accomplished your daily task, go to sleep in peace. God is awake.

—VICTOR HUGO

Sorrow is a fruit; God does not allow it to grow on a branch that is too weak to bear it.

—VICTOR HUGO

Never forget that [God] tests his real friends more severely than the lukewarm ones.

—KATHRYN HULME

Dear God: Help me get up. I can fall down by myself.

—JEWISH SAYING

He said not: thou shalt not be troubled, thou shalt not be tempted, thou shalt not be distressed. But he said thou shalt not be overcome.

—JULIAN OF NORWICH

I have always believed that God never gives us a cross to bear larger than we can carry. No matter what, he wants us to be happy, not sad. Birds sing after a storm. Why shouldn't we?

—ROSE KENNEDY

A season of suffering is a small price to pay for a clear view of God.

—MAX LUCADO

Afflictions are but the shadow of God's wings.

—GEORGE MACDONALD

A very large amount of human suffering and frustration is caused by the fact that many men and women are not content to be the sort of being that God has made them, but try to persuade themselves that they are really beings of some different kind.

—ERIC MASCALL

The highest joy to the Christian almost always comes through suffering. No flower can bloom in paradise which is not transplanted from Gethsemane.

—IAN MCLAREN

Earth hath no sorrow that heaven cannot heal.

—THOMAS MOORE

Once you become aware that the main business that you are here for is to know God, most of life's problems fall into place of their own accord.

—J. I. PACKER

God does not offer us a way out of the testings of life. He offers us a way through, and that makes all the difference.

—W. T. PURKISER

Grace grows best in the winter.

—SAMUEL RUTHERFORD

Believe in dreams. Never believe in hurts. . . . You can't let the grief and the hurts and the breaking experiences of life control your future decisions.

—ROBERT H. SCHULLER

The Lord gets his best soldiers out of the highlands of affliction.

—CHARLES HADDON SPURGEON

Sometimes God sends his love letters in black-edged envelopes. He allows us to taste the bitterness of want and the desolation of bereavement. . . . When there is no one at hand to say it to you, say it to yourself, "God is faithful, who will not suffer the pain to exceed the measure of my endurance."

—CHARLES HADDON SPURGEON

If God would make manifest the fact the "He giveth songs in the night," he must first make it night.

—WILLIAM TAYLOR

Christ came and he did not really explain [suffering]: he did far more. He met it, willed it, transformed it, and he taught us how to do all this, or rather he himself does it within us, if we do not hinder his all-healing hands.

—FRIEDRICH VON HÜGEL

How else but through a broken heart
May Lord Christ enter in?

—OSCAR WILDE

Where there is sorrow, there is holy ground.

—OSCAR WILDE

God gives burdens, also shoulders.

—YIDDISH PROVERB

See also God's Provision; Grace

TEMPTATION ∾

The enemy will wait forty years, if necessary, to set a trap for you.

—JOE ALDRICH

Though the bird may fly over your head, let it not make its nest in your hair.

—DANISH PROVERB

Not all that tempts your wand'ring eyes
And heedless hearts, is lawful prize;
Nor all that glisters, gold.

—THOMAS GRAY

What makes resisting temptation difficult, for many people, is that they don't want to discourage it completely.

—FRANKLIN P. JONES

The tempter, ever on the watch, wages war most violently against those whom he sees most careful to avoid sin.

—St. Leo the Great

If millions of Christians can be tempted to neglect the church, the scriptures, prayer and other dynamics of spiritual life, they can be kept at a subsistence level of strength which will offer little threat to the kingdom of evil.

—Richard F. Lovelace

As we go up the scale of spiritual excellence, temptation follows us all the way, becoming more refined as our lives are more refined, more subtle as our spiritual sensitiveness is keener.

—A. Victor Murray

'Tis one thing to be tempted, Escalus, another thing to fall.

—William Shakespeare, *Measure for Measure*

A man is led the way he wishes to follow.

—The Talmud

Temptation rarely comes in working hours. It is in their leisure time that men are made or marred.

—W. M. Taylor

O Christ, guide and strengthen all who are tempted in this hour.

—United Society for the Propagation of the Gospel

If you have been tempted into evil, fly from it. It is not falling into the water, but lying in it, that drowns.

—Unknown

The devil only tempts those souls that wish to abandon sin and those who are in a state of grace. The others belong to him; he has no need to tempt them.

—JOHN VIANNEY

I can resist everything except temptation.

—OSCAR WILDE

No degree of temptation justifies any degree of sin.

—NATHANIEL PARKER WILLIS

Ever notice that the whisper of temptation can be heard farther than the loudest call to duty?

—EARL WILSON

He who loves praise loves temptation.

—THOMAS WILSON

The devil never tempts us with more success than when he tempts us with a sight of our own good actions.

—THOMAS WILSON

See also Satan; Sin and Sinners

WAITING ❧

We must wait for God, long, meekly, in the wind and wet, in the thunder and lightning, in the cold and dark. Wait, and he will come. He never comes to those who do not wait.

—FREDERICK WILLIAM FABER

God may seem slow but he's never late.

—ROY LESSIN

When you don't know what to do, *wait!* God never panics and is never under pressure.

—ROY LESSIN

Waiting does not mean doing nothing. It is not fatalistic resignation. It means going about our assigned tasks, confident that God will provide the meaning and the conclusions. It is not compelled to work away at keeping up appearances with a bogus spirituality. It is the opposite of desperate and panicky manipulations, of scurrying and worrying.

—EUGENE PETERSON

More mistakes are probably made by speed than by sloth, by impatience than by dilatoriness. God's purposes often ripen slowly. If the door is shut, don't put your shoulder to it. Wait till Christ takes out the key and opens it.

—JOHN STOTT

Quiet waiting before God would save from many a mistake and from many a sorrow.

—JAMES HUDSON TAYLOR

See also God's Will; Guidance; Work and Vocation

WORK & VOCATION ∼

Vocation is not the exceptional prerogative of a few specially good or gifted people. . . . All men and women are called to serve God.

—F. R. BARRY

And first of all, whatever good work you begin to do, beg of him with most earnest prayer to perfect it.

—ST. BENEDICT

Ambition tyrannizes over our souls.

—ROBERT BURTON

Our grand business is not to see what lies dimly at a distance but to do what lies clearly at hand.

—THOMAS CARLYLE

It is better to wear out than rust out.

—RICHARD CUMBERLAND

No man can become a saint in his sleep.

—HENRY DRUMMOND

Have thy tools ready. God will find thee work.

—CHARLES KINGSLEY

If you are miserable or bored in your work . . . or dread going to it . . . then God is speaking to you. He either wants you to change the job you are in—or—more likely—he wants to change *you*.

—BRUCE LARSON

If he [God] has work for me to do I cannot die.

—HENRY MARTYN

The things, good Lord, that we pray for, give us the grace to labor for.

—THOMAS MORE

The awareness of a need and the capacity to meet that need: this constitutes a call.

—JOHN RALEIGH MOTT

Readiness and ability for any work is not given before the work, but only through the work.

—ANDREW MURRAY

Never feel above an honorable calling, nor be afraid of the coarse frock or apron. Put your hands to work in the line of duty; dust on your garments or moisture on your brow neither shame nor disgrace. Better soil your hands than your character.

—DANIEL ORCUTT,
MEMBER OF THE SHAKER COMMUNITY

No Christian should ever think or say that he is not fit to be God's instrument, for that in fact is what it means to be a Christian.

—ALAN PATON

Good deeds are the best prayer.

—SERBIAN PROVERB

God's work done in God's way will never lack God's supplies.

—JAMES HUDSON TAYLOR

Many people mistake our work for our vocation. Our vocation is the love of Christ.

—MOTHER TERESA

Your vocation is not to work for lepers. . . . Your vocation is to belong to Jesus.

—MOTHER TERESA

The meaning of man's work is the satisfaction of the instinct for adventure that God has implemented in his heart.

—PAUL TOURNIER

Ambition destroys its possessors.

—UNKNOWN

Ask God's blessing on your work but do not also ask him to do it.

—UNKNOWN

God doesn't give us the jobs we're fit for, he fits us for the jobs he gives us.

—UNKNOWN

Whatever is to be done at God's command may be accomplished in his strength.

—UNKNOWN

God's strength behind you, his concern for you, his love within you, and his arms beneath you are more than sufficient for the job ahead of you.

—WILLIAM ARTHUR WARD

WORSHIP

Worship is the overflow of the heart that asks nothing of God.

—CARL ARMERDING

A Christian should be an alleluia from head to foot.

—ST. AUGUSTINE

Christian worship is the most momentous, the most urgent, the most glorious action that can take place in human life.

—KARL BARTH

Worship is transcendent wonder.

—THOMAS CARLYLE

Do not hurry when you leave a place of worship.

—JOSEPH CARO

Then someone said, "Oh-oh! Time for the worship service." We all filed over to the vesper circle, the organ came on with its tremolo, and we sang some songs about our souls. That was supposed to be "worship." But it wasn't!

—HARVEY COX

You don't have to be afraid of praising God too much; unlike humans he never gets a big head.

—PAUL DIBBLE

Does anyone have the foggiest idea what sort of power we [Christians] so blithely invoke? Or, as I suspect, does no one believe a word of it? The churches are children playing on the floor with their chemistry sets, mixing up a batch of TNT to kill a Sunday morning. It is madness to wear ladies' straw hats and velvet hats to church; we should all be wearing crash helmets. Ushers should issue life preservers and signal flares; they should lash us to our pews. For the sleeping god may wake someday and take offense, or the waking god may draw us out to where we can never return.

—ANNIE DILLARD, *TEACHING A STONE TO TALK*

We don't need fasten-your-seatbelt signs in our pews because we no longer fly. We're like a group of geese attending meetings every Sunday where we talk passionately about flying and then get up and walk home.

—TIM HANSEL

The life that is too busy for worship is busier than God intended it to be. Work is life's eminent duty but worship is life's pre-eminent dynamic. To divorce one from the other is to court disaster, for while work exhausts power worship renews it.

—STUART HOLDEN

A man can no more diminish God's glory by refusing to worship him than a lunatic can put out the sun by scribbling the word "darkness" on the wall.

—C. S. LEWIS

Worship is one thing and entertainment is another, and it is dangerous business to play lightly with holy things, to tickle the senses in place of calling men to bow their hearts in faith and repentance.

—JOHN C. NEVILLE

A people's lives are only as good as their worship.

—EUGENE PETERSON

Worship does not satisfy our hunger for God—it whets our appetite. Our need for God is not taken care of by engaging in worship—it deepens.

—EUGENE PETERSON

Worship is an *act* which develops feelings for God, not a *feeling* for God which is expressed in an act of worship. . . .

—EUGENE PETERSON

The worship most acceptable to God comes from a thankful and cheerful heart.

—PLUTARCH

If the order of your worship service is so rigid that it can't be changed, it had better be changed.

—THEODORE A. RAEDEKE

I believe a very large majority of churchgoers are merely unthinking, slumbering worshipers of an unknown God.

—CHARLES HADDON SPURGEON

Millions are merely backseat Christians, willing to be observers of a performance which the professionals put on, ready to criticize or to applaud, but not willing even to consider the possibility of real participation.

—ELTON TRUEBLOOD

Worship as if thou wert to die today.

—TUSCAN

A pastor's prayer: "Do something for us today that isn't in the bulletin."

—UNKNOWN

Can we expect the flames of our worship of God to burn brightly in public on the Lord's Day when they barely flicker for him in secret on other days? Isn't it because we do not worship well in private that our corporate worship experience often dissatisfies us?

—DONALD WHITNEY

Our going to church on Sunday is like placing one's ear to another's chest to hear the unquenchable murmur of the human heart.

—RICHARD WRIGHT

AUTHOR INDEX

Swift, Jonathan, 136
Swindoll, Charles, 76, 90, 121
Swing, William, 153

Tagore, Rabindranath, 109
Talmud, the, 93, 157, 172
Taylor, Barbara Brown, 116
Taylor, James Hudson, 65, 119, 174, 176
Taylor, Jeremy, 91, 126, 130, 158
Taylor, Richard, 144
Taylor, W. M., 138, 172
Taylor, William, 170
Teilhard de Chardin, Pierre, 102, 106
Temple, William, 36, 37, 59, 143, 146
Templeton, Charles B., 37
ten Boom, Betsie, 69
ten Boom, Corrie, 59, 87, 158
Tennyson, Alfred, Lord, 44, 127
Teresa, Mother, 85, 99, 102, 106, 151, 176
Teresa of Avila, 158
Tertullian, 30, 109, 136
Theologica Germanica, 83
Thiessen, Evelyn A., 116
Thomas, George, 134
Thomas, Howard, 160
Thomas, W. Ian, 117
Thoreau, Henry David, 22
Tillich, Paul, 76
Tolstoy, Leo, 27, 28, 90
Torrey, R. A., 127, 151
Tournier, Paul, 49, 55, 106, 176
Tov, Israel Baal Shem, 90, 94

Tozer, A. W., 43, 65, 76, 80, 87, 104, 110, 117, 127, 148
Trench, Richard Chenevix, 127
Trobisch, Walter, 153
Trueblood, Elton, 37, 49, 55, 112, 180
Tuscan, 180
Tutu, Desmond, 37, 160
Twain, Mark, 19, 59, 127, 132

Ullathorne, William F., 16
Underhill, Evelyn, 22, 43, 85, 102
United Society for the Propagation of the Gospel, 56, 172
Unknown, 16, 22, 23, 28, 37, 39, 41, 45, 55, 56, 59, 65, 70, 80, 81, 82, 85, 88, 91, 95, 96, 99, 112, 117, 127, 130, 132, 136, 143, 148, 158, 164, 172, 176, 177, 180
Updike, John, 37, 153

Van Dyke, Henry, 134
van Gogh, Vincent, 99
vander Hoven, William, 102
Vann, Gerald, 85
Venard, Theophane, 102
Vianney, John, 173
Villa, Anthony Dalla, 117
Virgil, 83
Voltaire, 19, 65, 112
von Goethe, Johann Wolfgang, 91
von Grumbach, Argula, 19
von Hügel, Friedrich, 171
von Mises, Ludwig, 136

ABOUT THE AUTHOR

GORDON STUART JACKSON is the Associate Dean for Academic Affairs at Whitworth College, in Spokane, WA. He was raised in South Africa, where he worked as a journalist before receiving his doctorate from the School of Journalism at Indiana University in 1983. *Quotes for the Journey* is his third book.